W9-CSQ-906

WHAT SHALL WE SAY?

What Shall We Say?

Evil, Suffering, and the
Crisis of Faith

Thomas G. Long

WILLIAM B. EERDMANS PUBLISHING COMPANY

GRAND RAPIDS, MICHIGAN / CAMBRIDGE, U.K.

Published 2011 by

Wm. B. Eerdmans Publishing Co.

2140 Oak Industrial Drive N.E., Grand Rapids, Michigan 49505 /

P.O. Box 163, Cambridge CB3 9PU U.K.

Printed in the United States of America

17 16 15 14 13 12 11   7 6 5 4 3 2 1

Library of Congress Cataloging-in-Publication Data

Long, Thomas G., 1946-

What shall we say?: evil, suffering, and the crisis of faith / Thomas G. Long.

p.   cm.

"This book began as the 2009 Thomas White Currie lectures at Austin

Presbyterian Theological Seminary in Austin, Texas" — Acknowledgments.

Includes bibliographical references. 48220213

ISBN 978-0-8028-6514-4 (cloth: alk. paper)   3/12

1. Theodicy. 2. Doctrinal preaching.   I. Title.

BT160.L68   2011

231'.8 — dc22

2011009863

www.eerdmans.com

To the memory of my mother, Belle Smith Long,

and in thanksgiving for my granddaughters,

Carly, Rebekah, Belle, and Eva.

"My cup overflows." (Ps. 23:5)

Contents

Acknowledgments

⁓

This book began as the 2009 Thomas White Currie Lectures at Austin Presbyterian Theological Seminary in Austin, Texas. To participate in such a distinguished series, which includes in its lineage H. Richard Niebuhr's classic *Christ and Culture,* was more than an honor. It was a thrill. I am grateful to Dr. Theodore Wardlaw, Austin's president and a dear friend of long standing; to Dean Michael Jinkins, now president of Louisville Presbyterian Theological Seminary; to my kind hosts, Professor David White and his wife, Melissa Wiginton; and to all of the many others in Austin who made the seminary campus a place of hospitality and welcome. I am also grateful to the members of the Tom Currie Bible Class of the Highland Park Presbyterian Church in Dallas, Texas. They are not only the longtime sponsors of the Currie Lectures; they also provided me a Saturday evening feast and a Sunday morning forum to try out a few ideas from the lectures.

Subsequently, the lectures were adapted and delivered at the Closterhouse Colloquium at Northminster Presbyterian Church in Indianapolis, where the pastor, Dr. Teri Thomas, and the Closterhouse Committee, chaired by the ever-gracious Jean Dodds, provided far more care and encouragement than I deserved. Additionally, versions of these lectures were delivered as the 2010 Nicholson Lectures at the Atlantic School of Theology in Halifax, Nova Scotia. I am grateful to the school's president, the Reverend Canon Eric Beresford, for the kind invitation to be a part of this distinguished series, and to Dr. Laurence DeWolfe, professor of pastoral theology, for his generous hosting of me and for using his preacher's gift to regale me with wonderful stories.

My editor, Roger VanHarn, has been my friend and conversation partner about preaching for many years. I am grateful to him for guiding this project forward, and I want to thank Bill Eerdmans and the good team at Eerdmans Publishing Company for the wonderful support they have provided.

I wish as well to express my gratitude to Dean Jan Love and my other colleagues at Candler School of Theology at Emory University. The intellectual ethos of Candler is a constant and encouraging stimulus to rigorous, faithful, and creative scholarship. In particular, I wish to thank Carl Holladay, Luke Timothy Johnson, Steven J. Kraftchick, Joy Ann McDougall, Carol Newsom, Gail O'Day (now dean of the Wake Forest University School of Divinity), Karen Scheib, and Andrea White, colleagues whose writings and whose theological conversations with me are reflected in the ideas in these pages, even if they may not always recognize them. My research assistant, Sarah Reddish, has provided great help in preparing the manuscript.

An earlier version of the chapter of this book titled "Interlude: Howl: Job and the Whirlwind" appeared as "Job: Second Thoughts in the Land of Uz" in *Theology Today* 45, no. 1 (April 1988): 5-20. It is used here by permission.

Preface

In Archibald MacLeish's Pulitzer prize-winning play *J.B.,* two workers at a fleabag circus, a "Mr. Zuss," who sells balloons, and "Nickles," who is a popcorn vendor, mount a deserted sideshow stage and, after some hesitation, decide to act out the biblical story of Job. Zuss will play the part of God; Nickles will be Satan. What about the character of Job, the agonized sufferer? The two men observe wryly that there is always some human being to play Job.

Nickles begins to recite a little poem, naming the theme that will serve as the main challenge of the play:

> I heard upon his dry dung heap
> That man cry out who could not sleep:
> "If God is God He is not good;
> If God is good He is not God."[1]

MacLeish wrote *J.B.* in the mid-1950s, in response to the devastations of two world wars and the other horrors of the twentieth century, and his play sparked a conversation among playgoers and in the popular media about the character of God. Is God good? If so, given the scope of suffering, can we think of God as all-powerful?

1. Archibald MacLeish, *J.B.: A Play in Verse* (New York: Houghton Mifflin, 1989), p. 11.

These questions, taken together, have been called the "theodicy problem." As theological terms go, *theodicy* is a relative newcomer, having been invented by the philosopher Leibniz only three hundred years ago. Etymologically, the word *theodicy* is formed by gluing together two Greek words, *theos* (God) and *dikē* (justice), and in its original sense it meant "the justification of God." In a world where terrible catastrophes happen and where people suffer out of all proportion to any sense of deserving, God, it was felt, had some explaining to do. The ways of God needed to be justified. God needed a good defense, and theodicy was the enterprise of coming up with one.

This book is about what preachers can and should say regarding the theodicy problem. Engaging theodicy in the older sense of the word is not my goal, and providing a justification for the actions of God is not what I imagine myself to be doing in these pages. Indeed, to think that one could somehow defend God is theologically an act of extreme hubris. If God needs to be defended, God will need a better attorney than I.

More recently, though, theodicy has come to have a somewhat different meaning, one that is less about putting God on trial and more about putting our faith to the test. In this newer sense, which is the concern of this book, theodicy is about how believers can hold together important faith claims that seem, on the surface anyway, to be incompatible: that there is a God, that God is loving and just, that God is powerful, and that there is undeserved suffering in the world. Understood this way, theodicy is not about coming up with excuses for God's behavior in a world of evil but about how faith in a loving God is plausible, given what we know and experience about suffering.

It is no accident that the term *theodicy* is of more recent coinage than other theological concepts, such as "hope" and "salvation" and "sin." Only under the intellectual conditions of the modern (and now, perhaps, postmodern) world could the question of theodicy arise in its current forms. With the advent of modern science and of the idea of human reason as a counterforce to "revealed religion," new ways of thinking developed about such questions as how the universe is built and why natural disasters occur. If a volcano erupts, is this an act of God or simply the consequence of the buildup of gasses? If people are killed by the flow of lava, is this divine punishment, the operation of the indifferent laws of nature, or something else? After the Enlightenment, wondering why God doesn't intervene to stop suffering led inevitably to wondering if there even was a God to intervene at all.

Bishop Berkeley famously said that philosophers are people who kick up dust and then complain that they cannot see. Indeed, some suggest that worrying about the theodicy question is not a proper activity for Christian theology because the very issues at stake have been corrupted from the outset by Enlightenment philosophers. To ask "How could there be a God who is loving and just in a world of evil and suffering?" in the way that the problem has been posed for the last three centuries is already to be working with conceptions of "God," "love," "justice," and all the rest that are foreign to Christian faith. If Voltaire or David Hume couldn't see how it was possible for a good God to exist in a world of such evil, then perhaps it was because they had kicked up a load of dust and were working with the wrong ideas about "God," "good," and "evil."

Maybe so, but for many intellectually alert Christians today, the theodicy problem poses a deep challenge to their faith, and preachers do not have the luxury of dismissing in the pulpit a serious question that arises from the pews. It is not easy to understand how it is possible to say "I believe in God, the maker of heaven and earth" and "God is love" while, at the same time, having to say "My neighbor's daughter was born with severe brain damage" or "Over 200,000 people lost their lives in the earthquake in Haiti." This book, then, is a work of homiletical pastoral care. It is an attempt to stand with preachers, who then will stand with their parishioners, in thinking through how faith in a loving God holds together with the facts of life in a suffering world.

Here is how the book is arranged:

In Chapter 1, I describe how the question of theodicy, as we understand it today, arose in the intellectual history of the West. In Chapter 2, I explore how this problem, once the preoccupation of an elite cadre of eighteenth-century philosophers, has now been "democratized" and has become an active challenge to the faith of ordinary church people in our time, especially the most thoughtful members of our flocks.

Many theologians have tried, for good and various reasons, to shoo us away from the theodicy problem, to warn that theodicy is a theological Sargasso Sea in which no good ship of faith can survive. In Chapter 3,

I present these warnings, heed them partly, but also indicate why preachers do not finally have the luxury of avoiding urgent theological questions arising from the pews and must, therefore, sail ahead. In Chapter 4, I interrogate representative thinkers who have ventured their own responses to the theodicy problem, learning from them all but also challenging each of their "solutions."

The sequence of these initial chapters leads us inexorably to the place where we must at last articulate the goal of the book: what preachers can and should say about theodicy. This is the task I take up in Chapter 5, and I employ Jesus' parable of the wheat and the weeds as a resource and a guide. No exploration of theodicy, however, can avoid engaging the greatest "theodicy" text in Scripture, the book of Job. So, in an interlude between Chapters 4 and 5, I explore the theological implications of that magnificent and enigmatic story.

After some debate, I decided not to include sample sermons on theodicy in this book. Example sermons can be useful, of course, but when it comes to the theodicy problem, the questions are so many, the issues so complex, the possible approaches so varied, that one or two sermonic examples would, in my view, be more misleading than helpful. Readers curious about what a good theodicy sermon would look like can, however, look in two directions for help. First, good anthologies of sermons on various aspects of the theodicy question are available, such as *This Incomplete One: Words Occasioned by the Death of a Young Person,* ed. Michael D. Bush (Grand Rapids: Eerdmans, 2006). Second, the presentation of the parable of the wheat and the weeds in Chapter 5 is intended to be "sermon-like," to embody what a preacher might say in a sermon on that text, albeit in expanded form.

One of my mentors in homiletics, the fine Lutheran preacher Edmund Steimle, said in a seminar that a good sermon "is never a neat package tied up with a bow. Rather, a good sermon is like rings on the surface of a lake where a swimmer has gone down in deep water." My hope for this little book, then, is that it will mark the deep water in the lake and invite other preachers to take the plunge.

Candler School of Theology   THOMAS G. LONG
Emory University, Atlanta, Georgia

CHAPTER ONE

The Shaking of the Foundations

&

"If God exists, who needs enemies? . . . I'll take Aphrodite, or Lady Luck."

Letter to the editor, *New York Times*[1]

Here is an ordinary diary with a startling entry:

There never was a finer morning seen than the 1st of November; the sun shone out in its full luster; the whole face of the sky was perfectly serene and clear; and not the least signal of warning of that approaching event, which has made this once flourishing, opulent, and populous city, a scene of the utmost horror and desolation. . . .[2]

What city and what "utmost horror" are being described here? If the diary had referred to August 6, we might have guessed Hiroshima. If it

1. From a letter to the editor in response to Stanley Fish's essay "Suffering, Evil, and the Existence of God," *The New York Times*, 4 November 2007, and available at http://opinionator.blogs.nytimes.com/2007/11/04/suffering-evil-and-the-existence-of-god.

2. From *Italy, France, Spain, and Portugal*, vol. 5 of *The World's Story: A History of the World in Story, Song, and Art*, 14 vols. (Boston: Houghton Mifflin, 1914), p. 618.

WHAT SHALL WE SAY?

had read "September 11," we would have named New York. "January 12," and it would have been Port-au-Prince. But the day was November 1, and this is the account of a local merchant who had the misfortune to be in Lisbon, Portugal, on that dreadful day in 1755, when at 9:40 in the morning all hell broke loose and the world seemed to have come to an apocalyptic end.

November 1 is All Saints' Day. It was a holy day in Lisbon, and most of the population was in church that morning. In the mid-eighteenth century, Lisbon was one of Europe's most religious and pious cities, a center of archly conservative Roman Catholicism. Of its 250,000 residents, fully 25,000 of them, one out of every ten citizens, were priests or monks or nuns.[3] Historian Charles Boxer says that Portugal in that time, Lisbon included, had more priests per capita than any other nation on earth, with the possible exception of Tibet.[4]

But Lisbon's religion was, in many ways, a leftover medieval piety. Woven into the fabric of the devotion was a dark dread of the Day of Wrath, a sense of personal and social sinfulness and the always impending judgment of God. For two hundred years, Lisbon had served as the headquarters of the Holy Office of the Inquisition, the foreboding and stern face of the church, devoted to rooting out and punishing heresy. Thousands had been burned at the stake, imprisoned, banished, or sentenced to galley slavery. It was not uncommon to see marching through the streets of Lisbon bands of penitents hoping to show for all to see their devotion, flailing themselves with whips and chains, beating their breasts in remorse for their sins, and crying out, "Penitence! Penitence!" Lisbon desired not only to be devout, but also to be pure.

But it was never enough. Lisbon's God was a jealous God, and the prophecy of doom was ever in the air. As Nicholas Shrady has observed,

> For as long as anyone could remember, soothsayers and diviners, pamphleteers and prognosticators, clerics and ascetics had been preaching unequivocal doom for the Portuguese capital. The signs and portents, they insisted, were varied, if unmistakable —

3. Nicholas Shrady, *The Last Day: Wrath, Ruin, and Reason in the Great Lisbon Earthquake of 1755* (New York: Viking, 2008), p. 10.
4. Charles R. Boxer, as cited in Shrady, *The Last Day,* p. 11.

a rash of stillborn infants, a comet streaking the heavens, the feverish dreams of a cloistered nun, a vision of avenging angels hovering over the city — and they all pointed to Lisbon's destruction at the hands of a wrathful God.[5]

What the prophets of doom could not agree on was just how this destruction of Lisbon would take place. Some said by earthquake, others said by wind, some warned of fire, and still others presaged flood. As it turns out, they were much too modest. Lisbon's day of hell included the catastrophic forces of all four.

At about 9:30 that morning, a massive earthquake convulsed the ocean floor some sixty miles out in the North Atlantic, and the tremors rippled with fearsome force toward the city. The churches of the city were packed, especially the church of the city's patron saint, the Basilica of Saint Vincent, where the crowds filled every available space, spilling down the front steps and into the square. Just as the priests intoned *"Gaudeamus omnes in Domino, diem festum"* ("Let us all rejoice in the Lord on this festival day!"), the walls of St. Vincent's began to shake violently. The bell towers swayed like reeds in a wind, their bells clanging wildly. Candle stands fell to the floor; shards of stained glass exploded onto the terrified worshipers; panicked priests fled from the altar. Some worshipers stayed in place, praying for mercy, while others fled into the streets, to be met by the crowds streaming in terror from other churches and buildings. They got there just in time for the second, and stronger, shock wave (about a 7.0 on the Richter scale, scientists today estimate), which toppled buildings and demolished the city. Churches, homes, and government buildings collapsed on the crowds in the streets, killing thousands of people instantly, leaving others bleeding and wounded. The dust stirred up turned the sky black, and all across the city could be heard the sounds of weeping and cries of "Mercy, dear God, mercy!"

But there was no mercy. Fires, many of them started by fallen candles in the churches, were being fanned by strange and howling winds that whipped brutally through the city, and, as if that were not enough, minutes later a third shock wave passed through the city. By now, there

5. Shrady, *The Last Day*, p. 1.

was hardly anything left standing to destroy. With the city ablaze and the land now littered with rubble and corpses, dazed survivors instinctively made their way toward the River Tagus, toward the water, toward what seemed to be the only safe place left, the harbor. But like the "beast rising out of the sea" in the book of Revelation, this evil thing was not done with the people of Lisbon, and it seemed to pursue them with a malevolent intelligence. As thousands stood on the wharf, hoping to board ships and flee the devastation of the burning city, according to some accounts, the water was suddenly and mysteriously sucked out of the harbor, dragging ships out to sea and revealing old shipwrecks and refuse on the now-waterless harbor floor. As the people stood dumbstruck by this latest omen, they looked up and discovered where the harbor water had gone: a mountain of ocean water, a tsunami, summoned to massive height by the concussion of the earthquake, was heading toward them. Almost before they could register their alarm, the huge wall of water obliterated them, and thousands more were drowned in the sudden surge.

No one knows for certain how many people died in Lisbon on that All Saints' Day. Some say 15,000; others say as many as 50,000 or 60,000. What is known is that the bodies of the victims floated in the harbor for weeks.

The Aftershocks

The seismic shock waves that destroyed Lisbon were soon followed by moral and theological shock waves that shook the intellectual, philosophical, and religious foundations of Europe and the West, and continue to shake them to this day. Historian Thomas D. Kendrick called the Lisbon earthquake "a disaster that had shocked Western civilization more than any other event since the fall of Rome in the fifth century,"[6] and philosopher Susan Neiman said, "The eighteenth century used the word *Lisbon* much as we use the word *Auschwitz* today. . . . It takes no

6. Thomas Downing Kendrick, *The Lisbon Earthquake* (New York: Lippincott, 1957), p. 185.

more than the name of a place to mean: the collapse of the most basic trust in the world. . . ."[7]

It is clear why the Lisbon earthquake turned the city to rubble, but why is this one calamity of such magnitude in the cultural and intellectual history of the West? It was not as if the world had never before experienced a natural disaster. Cataclysms and catastrophes have always been a part of human experience. Devastating earthquakes had happened before, and Lisbon, in fact, was no stranger to them. Nor was it a matter of scale. In terms of the magnitude of terror and the sheer loss of life, the Black Plague was far more calamitous than any earthquake, including Lisbon's. Recurring in waves over two centuries, the Black Plague was "one of the greatest biomedical catastrophes in human history,"[8] a vicious epidemic that wiped out a third of the population of Europe. The Black Death struck with fearful swiftness, taking people from health to the grave in a matter of hours. The Italian writer Boccaccio said that the victims of the Black Death "having breakfasted in the morning with their kinsfolk, acquaintances, and friends, supped that same evening with their ancestors in the next world!"[9]

But the All Saints' Day earthquake in Lisbon was different. It was a catastrophe that not only destroyed a city but also symbolized the destruction of a worldview. "At one particular moment in Europe . . . ," wrote Susan Neiman, "an earthquake could shake the foundations of faith and call the goodness of Creation into question."[10] The reason for this was a matter of timing. The Lisbon tragedy happened in the midst of a major turning point in human understanding, right in the middle of the breakup of the way that medieval society viewed the world and the emergence of a new set of assumptions about knowledge, reason, and nature — a time we have come to call the Enlightenment. The Lisbon earthquake, then, not only toppled churches, shops, and homes; it also symbolized the toppling of an old world and the way that world grasped faith and held on to hope.

7. Susan Neiman, *Evil in Modern Thought: An Alternative History of Philosophy* (Princeton: Princeton University Press, 2002), p. 1.

8. Mark Harrison, *Disease and the Modern World: 1500 to the Present Day* (Cambridge: Polity Press, 2004), p. 22.

9. Giovanni Boccaccio, *The Decameron* (New York: Penguin Classics, 2003), p. 13.

10. Neiman, *Evil in Modern Thought*, p. 246.

Prior to the Enlightenment, natural disasters such as earthquakes, famines, floods, and epidemics were viewed as coming directly from the hand of God. Fourteenth-century physicians who labored to stem the spread of the Black Death may have differed on the best practical treatments to employ on the victims — leeches? garlic necklaces? — but they agreed that God was the cause of all of the distress. They could debate what to do, but the issue of who made this epidemic happen was never in doubt.

Ever since Aristotle, people had assumed that, for something to exist, whether that something be a table, a person, or a plague, four ingredients — four "causes" — must be present: (1) the maker, (2) the form, (3) the material, and (4) the reason. A table, for example, doesn't just happen. Someone has to make it, according to some form or design, out of some material, and for some purpose. By the same logic, medieval society knew that the Black Death had a maker, a form, constituent material, and a reason for being made. As for the form of the disease and the material from which it was made, those were physical matters, questions of "nature," and therefore the physicians could debate them and experiment with various treatments. But when it came to the questions of who made this disease and for what reason, these were metaphysical questions, and the physicians, like virtually everyone else, nodded in assent to the answers of the theologians: God (or, for some, Satan) was the maker and the reason was punishment for sin.[11]

Magnus II, a king of Sweden who reigned in the fourteenth century at the height of the plague, spoke not only for himself but for the whole medieval culture: "God for the sins of men has struck this great punishment of sudden death. By it, most of our countrymen are dead."[12] Even two centuries later, the French royal surgeon and medical writer Ambroise Paré could still agree: "The plague is a malady come from God: furious, tempestuous, swift, monstrous, and frightful, contagious, terrible, fierce, treacherous, deceptive, mortal enemy of human life and that of many animals and plants."[13]

11. Joseph Patrick Byrne, *The Black Death* (Westport, Conn.: Greenwood Press, 2004), p. 38.
12. Byrne, *The Black Death*, p. 40.
13. Byrne, *The Black Death*, p. 40.

If God had caused the Black Death, then only God could stop it, and medical treatment for the plague was a strange combination of therapy and theology, a blend of practical, trial-and-error remedies (leeches, bloodletting, herbal poultices, isolation of the afflicted in "pesthouses") and prescribed acts of religious penitence. "The medieval world," notes historian Mark Harrison,

> ... was very different from our own, and the coming of the plague was interpreted very largely in the light of Catholic theology. As far as the Church was concerned, there was one obvious conclusion to be drawn from the plague: that God was punishing humanity for some form of wickedness. That wickedness and those responsible for it had to be identified and rooted out. . . . People were exhorted to acts of penance, pilgrimage, and propitiation, which included processions of flagellants which moved from town to town scourging their flesh with whips to remove the sins of humanity.[14]

Today, someone with a bad case of the flu would be shocked and probably offended if a physician were to say, "Take Tylenol every four hours, drink plenty of fluids, and say your prayers of confession, since God has caused this as a punishment for sin," but for medieval physicians, divine causality of disease was the water in which they swam. As Joseph Byrne observes, "Acceptance of metaphysical causes in addition to natural causes [for the plague] was not merely a matter of religious belief or adherence; it was a matter of accepting the philosophical framework that united the entire Western intellectual enterprise."[15]

By 1755, however, that philosophical framework was undergoing dramatic renovation. Symbolically, the Lisbon earthquake would be the first disaster of worldwide proportion that could not be neatly fit into the accepted idea of divine causality. The medieval intellectual synthesis, and along with it the accepted theology of the time, was colliding with new ways of thinking as violently as the undersea tectonic plates that precipitated the Lisbon disaster, and what was inexorably beginning to take

14. Harrison, *Disease and the Modern World*, pp. 23-24.
15. Byrne, *The Black Death*, p. 38.

shape, in Europe and elsewhere, was what we today call the "modern scientific worldview."

The deeper transformation of intellectual life may have come slowly and have been hidden from view, but on the surface the cultural changes were rapid and palpable, especially in natural science. In the hundred years prior to the Lisbon earthquake, telescopes and microscopes with complex systems of optics were developed, and human beings began to explore the vast reaches of the universe and the secret recesses of nature close at hand. The new breed of explorers called themselves "natural philosophers" (we would call them "scientists," but that term would not appear until early in the nineteenth century), and they employed the logic gained from philosophy to reason about what they were observing in nature. Their discoveries were staggering. For the first time, human blood cells were visible under the power of the microscope; the refracting telescope disclosed that Saturn had rings and a large moon; the principles of calculus were articulated; the rotational periods of Jupiter, Mars, and Venus were calculated; the mercury thermometer and the navigational sextant were invented; and Benjamin Franklin in America conducted his experiments with the mysterious force called "electricity."

What these natural philosophers were finding was not simply a collection of cells, planets, orbits, and lightning bolts, but much more: a world that seemed to operate on its own steam. Far from waiting on God to raise the sun each day, the world, from the smallest cell to the sweeping orbits of the planets, seemed to be self-regulating and appeared to work according to predictable principles and definable natural laws. In 1716, when perhaps the greatest of these natural philosophers, Isaac Newton, published the second edition of his groundbreaking *Philosophiæ Naturalis Principia Mathematica,* he could define time and space in these words: "Absolute, true, and mathematical time, of itself, and from its own nature, flows equably without relation to anything external, and by another name is called duration. . . . Absolute space, in its own nature, without regard to anything external, remains always familiar and unmovable."[16]

Notice that for Newton both time and space have their "own nature"

16. Isaac Newton, *The Mathematical Principles of Natural Philosophy* (London: H. D. Symonds, 1803), p. 6.

and can be defined without relation or regard "to anything external." This claim has staggering implications for theology, of course. If time, space, and presumably everything that moves within them can be defined without recourse to anything outside of them, then what is the role of God — or even the need for God? Newton was a religious man — a tad eccentric, perhaps, but religious nonetheless — and he was careful to say that the very design of the universe pointed to a creator. "We see the effects of a Deity in the creation," he wrote. The job of the natural philosopher is to observe the natural world and to consider it to be the visible effects of certain underlying causes. These causes are, in turn, the results of deeper causes, and the task is to keep unwinding the strands of cause and effect until they lead inevitably to God. "'Tis the business of this Philosophy to argue from the effects to their causes till we come at the first cause."[17]

Newton believed in an infinite, omnipotent, and all-wise God as surely as any Anglican divine; the difference with Newton was that he believed that the best proof of this God was not in a book of theology but in the grand, intricate, and beautiful design of nature itself.[18] Newton's devoted assistant, the mathematician Roger Cotes, agreed. In the preface to the second edition of Newton's *Principia,* he proclaimed in an exultant sentence something akin to the "intelligent design" argument for divine creation: "Without all doubt, this world, so diversified with that variety of forms and motions we find in it, could arise from nothing but the perfectly free will of God directing and presiding over all."

The fact that Newton, as well as many other seventeenth- and eighteenth-century natural philosophers, took pains to stand at the front door of the new house of scientific meaning and confess their faith in God and to proclaim loudly a belief in the divine creator tends to disguise the radical implications that their science held for the idea of God and for the understanding of God's relation to creation. The psalms of praise at the front door finally could not drown out the laments of doubt beginning to be chanted at the back door. At the very least, a God defined as the philosophical "first cause" in a long chain of causal interactions, a God who

17. Isaac Newton, *Opticks,* 2d ed. (London: William Innys, 1717), p. 344.

18. Stephen D. Snobelen, "Isaac Newton: His Science and Religion," in *Science, Religion, and Society: An Encyclopedia of History, Culture, and Controversy,* vol. 1, ed. Arri Eisen and Gary Laderman (Armonk, N.Y.: M. E. Sharpe, 2007), p. 364.

could be described as "directing and presiding over all," was a very different God than either the God spoken of in Scripture or the God of medieval piety. The God of the Bible walked in the Garden of Eden in the cool of the day, appeared amid smoke and seraphim to Isaiah in the temple, and sent the angel Gabriel to visit the Virgin Mary. The God who serves as the first cause in a universe of planets, moons, and comets spinning along their mathematically predictable orbits according to natural laws was more like the designer of a power plant, content now to monitor the dials and gauges, intervening only to keep the system running smoothly.

One way to describe this theological change is that the doctrine of particular providence was yielding to the doctrine of general providence. Particular providence involves the claim that God is an active player in the specific events and circumstances of the world. God is involved in abundant harvest and in famine; God sends illness and health; God answers prayer and calls people to speak and act; God parts the sea for Moses, delivers the children of Israel from slavery, and raises Jesus from the dead. Indeed, the character and will of God are revealed in these "mighty acts" of particular providence. General providence, on the other hand, is the notion that God cares for the world not through extraordinary interventions of divine action but through constant and unchanging sustenance and the benevolent design of creation. If your architect neighbor comes to rescue you from your collapsing house in the middle of a gale, that's particular providence. If your architect friend doesn't have to come to rescue you because he has engineered your house to withstand the storm, that's general providence.

The more that natural philosophers like Newton discovered about the intricate, well-ordered, and intelligible design of the universe, the less need there was for God to intrude in the process — indeed, the less plausible such divine intrusions seemed. "If the universal scientific order is such a marvel," says Susan Neiman, "why suffer a God who kept jumping in and out of it? A Creation that was good in the beginning should require no intervention thereafter. Particular providence demanded too much meddling in the scientific order whose contemplation provided the Enlightenment with so much satisfaction."[19]

19. Neiman, *Evil in Modern Thought*, p. 246.

Another way this theological shift has been named is as the "disenchantment of the world." An enchanted world is one in which God (or the gods) is active in the events of everyday life. God is present in the falling rain, the breaking of bread at the dinner table, the kiss of lovers, the birth of a child, the wind in the trees. The skies sing of the glory of God, and the firmament proclaims the divine handiwork. A disenchanted world, on the other hand, is one in which the world is a closed system operating according to natural laws. God — if in fact there is a God — is outside the system, and, contrary to Newton's confidence, there is nothing in the natural order that demonstrates that the universe is, in fact, a divine creation. To the eyes of faith, the blooming of flowers and the spangling of stars in the night sky may be the fingerprints of God, but to others these events can be fully described in terms like cellular mitosis and thermonuclear fusion.

A half-century after the Lisbon disaster, a brilliant, if somewhat vain, natural philosopher by the name of Laplace published his book *Celestial Mechanics,* which was essentially a mathematical explanation of the workings of the universe. Convinced that no less a figure than Napoleon would be interested in his arguments, Laplace wangled an appointment with the emperor and presented him with a copy of the book. Napoleon, who had a fondness for asking embarrassing questions, had been tipped off that *Celestial Mechanics* contained not a single reference to God. So, as he received Laplace's gift of the book, he asked him, "Monsieur Laplace, they tell me you have written this large book on the system of the universe and have never even mentioned its creator." Laplace stiffened and huffed, "I have no need of that hypothesis."[20]

A disenchanted world, a world that has no need of the "hypothesis" of God, is a precondition for the kind of secularity characteristic of twenty-first-century society. We have moved, as philosopher Charles Taylor has put it,

> . . . from a society in which it was virtually impossible not to believe in God, to one in which faith, even for the staunchest believer, is one human possibility among others. I may find it incon-

20. Walter William Rouse Ball, *A Short Account of the History of Mathematics,* 4th ed. (London: Macmillan, 1908), p. 418.

ceivable that I would abandon my faith, but there are others, including possibly some very close to me, whose way of living I cannot in all honesty just dismiss as depraved, or blind, or unworthy, who have no faith (at least in God, or the transcendent). Belief in God is no longer axiomatic. There are alternatives.[21]

Most Christians today have learned to be bilingual, speaking the language of both enchantment and disenchantment. If it rains in the middle of a drought, we will say, "We needed that. God has blessed us with rain." Enchantment. But we will also watch the Weather Channel and know that this rain was caused by air with a certain level of humidity being cooled to a certain temperature. And it will rain every time this happens and not rain until it happens again. Disenchantment. Only with the Enlightenment and the disenchantment it entailed can we begin to speak of the world and God as separate realities — theism — or even of the natural world without God — atheism.

In 1755, culture was on the hinge between the old world of medieval piety and the new world of scientific secularity. The early natural scientists like Newton could plant a foot in both worlds. The universe was an elegant and mathematically complex natural system, but God was still around — omniscient and omnipotent, standing guard over the creation and ready to step in should anything go awry.

But then on November 1, something did go awry, terribly awry. And the awful question hung in the air: Where was God when the city of Lisbon, on its knees in prayer, was stalked down and destroyed?

Explaining Lisbon

At first, it seemed as though Lisbon changed nothing, especially for the church. Jesus himself had warned, "There will be wars and rumors of wars, . . . famines and earthquakes" (Matt. 24:6-7), and many Christian theologians and philosophers could take Lisbon in stride. The horrors of that day could be accounted for.

---

21. Charles Taylor, *A Secular Age* (Cambridge, Mass.: Belknap Press, 2007), p. 3.

As for the theologians, the well-worn explanations of the past were advanced once again. God had the whole world in his hands, and if the city of Lisbon had been destroyed, then it must have been the hands of God that had done the devastation, and for good reason. As Lisbon slowly rebuilt, Catholic preachers thundered that the earthquake had sprung from the will of God, that this tragedy was a call to all to repent, and that it was also a divine Inquisition of sorts and "had sent a great harvest of sinful souls . . . to hell."[22] Protestant preachers said that it was the hand of God all right, but a hand turned in wrath against Catholic Lisbon for its Romanish superstitions and popery. The earthquake, after all, had not destroyed Frankfurt or Geneva, but had worked its wrath during Mass in Lisbon.

News of the disaster traveled by ship all the way to the New World, to Boston, and a preacher in the colony of Massachusetts preached a series of sermons on the Lisbon disaster, naming one by one the sins that could provoke God to send a similar earthquake to the colony: avarice, pride, prodigality, deceit, and on and on. Charles Wesley even wrote a hymn explaining theologically what the Lisbon tragedy meant. He drew upon the imagery of Revelation 16 in which the "seventh angel" pours a bowl of wrath upon the earth, causing a violent earthquake. The first stanza reads:

Woe! To the men, on earth who dwell,
Nor dread th' Almighty frown,
When God doth all his wrath reveal,
And shower his judgments down!
Sinners, expect those heaviest showers,
To meet your God prepare,
When lo! The seventh angel pours
His vial in the air![23]

If the theologians interpreted Lisbon as the judgment of God upon sinful humanity, Christian philosophers, too, had their explanations for Lisbon. Forty years before the earthquake, the brilliant physicist, logician,

22. Shrady, *The Last Day,* p. 129.

23. Charles Wesley, "A Hymn on Revelation 16-17ff., Occasioned by the Destruction of Lisbon."

mathematician, and philosopher Gottfried Wilhelm Leibniz had written his persuasive and highly influential work called *Theodicy* — a word that Leibniz invented to describe the defense of the moral goodness of God. In this book, Leibniz claimed that this world, the actual world we live in, is the best of all possible worlds. God, the Creator, imagined an infinite number of alternative creations and then actualized the one possibility that most achieves God's moral purposes. This is the best world possible, and nothing could be different, down to the smallest detail, such as Leibniz could not have worn black socks on June 3, 1710, instead of the gray socks he actually wore. That would be a different world than we actually have, which is the one world allowable in the wisdom of God.[24]

Now, most people have at least a short list of ways that creation could be improved, imagining the world would actually have been a better place without, say, polio, Adolf Hitler, the AIDS virus, and Alzheimer's disease. But Leibniz claimed that God knows better than we do, that this different and supposedly better world we can imagine is not in fact the world that has the maximum possibility for perfection and goodness. What are apparently evils to us are actually, in terms of the totality of things, necessary conditions for God to bring this creation to a place of greater good. The sequence of Leibniz's argument is important. He does not look at the world and come to the conclusion that this is the "best of all possible" worlds. Rather, he begins with the view that God is good, holy, and just, and then reasons that this kind of God would have created nothing less than the best possible creation. Thus, Leibniz claims that we must come to the conclusion

> that there must have been great or rather invincible reasons which prompted the divine Wisdom to the permission of the evil that surprises us, from the mere fact that this permission has occurred: for nothing can come from God that is not altogether consistent with goodness, justice, and holiness. In God, this conclusion holds good: he did this, therefore he did it well.[25]

24. Maria Rosa Antognazza, *Leibniz: An Intellectual Biography* (Cambridge: Cambridge University Press, 2009), p. 485.

25. Gottfried Wilhelm Leibniz, *Theodicy: Essays on the Goodness of God, the Freedom of Man, and the Origin of Evil* (New Haven, Conn.: Yale University Press, 1952), p. 35.

But theological and philosophical explanations like Leibniz's were products of the old world, and people were now poised to find them implausible. It took the shock of Lisbon to tip the balance. After Lisbon, such arguments for the moral character of a God who could allow, much less cause, a disaster like that began to lose traction, first with philosophers and then with theologians. The disaster of Lisbon dramatically revealed the stress fractures in medieval thought and simply overwhelmed the ethical and theological categories that once could contain such catastrophes. The people of Lisbon were at prayer. They were praising God when the merciless disaster befell them. The devastation spared no one — rich or poor, pious or lapsed, good or bad. If an intelligence of any kind caused that terrible day, it was an intelligence whose bloodthirsty violence was random and promiscuous. If any moral will stood behind the events of Lisbon on All Saints' Day, it was a will whose cruelty was all out of proportion to any moral lesson it could possibly convey.

At first it was the Enlightenment philosophers who were bold enough to raise the challenging questions. Voltaire, for example, wrote a satire in which the main character, Candide, goes through the horrors of the Lisbon earthquake and its aftermath of judgment and "terrified, dumbfounded, bewildered, covered with blood, quivering from head to foot," takes a swipe at Leibniz when he says to himself: "If this is the best of all possible worlds, what are the others?"[26] As Theodor Adorno wrote, "The earthquake of Lisbon sufficed to cure Voltaire of the theodicy of Leibniz."[27]

Gradually theology as well was cured of the theodicy of Leibniz. Two hundred years before the Lisbon earthquake, the Heidelberg Catechism, written in an enchanted world, said this:

QUESTION 27: What do you understand by the providence of God?

ANSWER: The almighty and ever-present power of God whereby he still upholds, as it were by his own hand, heaven and earth together with all creatures, and rules in such a way that leaves and

26. Voltaire, *Candide, or Optimism,* chapter 6.
27. Theodor Adorno, *Negative Dialectics,* trans. E. B. Ashton (New York: Routledge, 1973), p. 361.

grass, rain and drought, fruitful and unfruitful years, food and drink, health and sickness, riches and poverty, and everything else, come to us not by chance but by his fatherly hand.

But in the eighteenth century, it was no longer easy for reasonable and thoughtful people to see the Lisbon horrors as the gift of God's "fatherly hand." The only God who could have promulgated such a cruel terror, who could have found any room in the divine will for such promiscuous suffering, was a moral monster.

Susan Neiman claims that Lisbon marks the birth of modernity, when the world began at last to grow up, to move away from theology and metaphysics and toward science and human responsibility. She finds that those thinkers in the eighteenth century who tried to scramble and repair that older theological worldview to be the product of "intellectual immaturity." She says, "If one believes the world is ruled by a good and powerful father figure, it's natural to expect his order to be comprehensibly just." But who could make a case for comprehensible justice in Lisbon? In the face of Lisbon, the whole idea of a good and powerful father God needed to be given up. "Jettison that belief" (that is, the belief in a wise and parental God), writes Neiman, "and whatever expectations remain are unresolved residues of childish fantasy. Thus the intellectual shock waves generated by Lisbon, when noticed at all, are seen as the birth pangs of a sadder but wiser era that has learned to live on its own."[28]

America had its own Lisbon a century later. Drew Gilpin Faust, in her brilliant book *The Republic of Suffering: Death and the Civil War,* claims that the typical religious views of nineteenth-century Americans about death and life, souls and bodies, and heaven and the nature of life eternal were simply not prepared for the mechanized slaughter and the overwhelming scale of death in the Civil War, with over 600,000 often dismembered bodies of the young lying in the fields of Virginia, Pennsylvania, Georgia, and Mississippi. Long before the terrorist attacks of September 11, 2001, the Civil War was America's crisis of faith. At the end of the Civil War, the Presbytery of South Carolina admitted that "the faith of

---

28. Neiman, *Evil in Modern Thought,* p. 5.

many a Christian is shaken by the mysterious and unlooked-for course of divine Providence." And one Southern woman wrote in her dairy that she felt "like a ship without a pilot or a compass," and there was no longer any God at the helm.[29]

Heirs of the philosophical changes in Europe, some educated nineteenth-century Americans experienced religious skepticism and doubt, and the devastations of the War accelerated and democratized this trend. As Gilpin Faust puts it: "Civil War carnage transformed the mid-nineteenth century's growing sense of religious doubt into a crisis of belief that propelled many Americans to redefine or reject their faith in a benevolent or responsive deity."[30]

Children of Lisbon

We are all the heirs of Lisbon. Many people in the pews of churches today, people who perhaps have never heard of the Lisbon earthquake of 1755, are nevertheless shaped powerfully by the turn in thought symbolized by that woeful day. What was once the outrageous thought of some philosophers of the eighteenth century and then became the daring skepticism of the educated elite in the nineteenth century has now become the common dilemma of the average person, including many of the people in our churches — namely, that belief in a loving and powerful God is deeply challenged by the irrationality and inexplicability of innocent suffering. Their faith is at best made more difficult by, and at worst is no match for, what has come to be known as the theodicy problem.

Years ago when I was seminary student, I was leading a congregation in Sunday worship, one of the first times I had been given that responsibility. When the service was over, I was standing at the door greeting the people, and a woman came up to me. She was, I knew, in a stressful and unhappy marriage, she was bedeviled herself by emotional problems, and she was the mother of two children with disabilities. Hers was a diffi-

29. Drew Gilpin Faust, *The Republic of Suffering: Death and the American Civil War* (New York: Alfred A. Knopf, 2008), p. 192.

30. Gilpin Faust, *The Republic of Suffering*, p. 210.

cult life. She took my hand, looked me in the eye, and said, "That was a great first hymn this morning."

Truthfully, I could not remember what the first hymn was, but she was so intense in her statement that some response was demanded. "Yes, it's certainly one of my favorites," I bluffed. Suddenly her expression darkened, and her face filled with disgust. I realized with a start that what she had said about the hymn being "great" had been dripping with sarcasm.

"Well, I thought it was an outrage!" She dropped my hand and marched away from the church. As soon as I could, I dashed back into the church and found a bulletin. The first hymn was "God Will Take Care of You." So believed the people of Lisbon.

It took two weeks for the news of Lisbon to reach most of the rest of Europe. Now, of course, there is a Lisbon a week on cable news. We see house fires that kill children in their sleep and tsunamis that take 200,000 lives, and the questions provoked by Lisbon three centuries ago are asked by almost every believer. When those of us who preach stand up on Sunday morning, we are looking out at many educated and thoughtful Christians who want to hang on to faith, but who secretly wonder — often silently, sometimes in ways denied and hidden even from themselves — if Susan Neiman is right about faith being a childish fantasy. With all that they know and see, they can no longer rest easily with the claim that the world is ruled by a good and powerful parental God, and so they wonder if the faith they are being asked to believe and live, the faith they want to believe and live, is simply a way of making us feel better in the storm, and if it is time to grow up and move on to a sadder but wiser world where we must stand up and be on our own.

CHAPTER TWO

The Impossible Chess Match

⌒*✓*⌒

[Ted Turner] was religious, and he decided that he was going to be a missionary. Then his sister became ill. He was fifteen when Mary Jane, who was twelve, contracted systemic lupus erythematosus, a disease in which the immune system attacks the body's tissue. She was racked with pain and constantly vomiting, and her screams filled the house. Ted regularly came home and held her hand, trying to comfort her. He prayed for her recovery; she prayed to die. After years of misery, she succumbed. Ted lost his faith. "I was taught that God was love and God was powerful," he says, "and I couldn't understand how someone so innocent should be made or allowed to suffer so."

Ken Auletta on Ted Turner in *The New Yorker*[1]

For Sisters Agnes and Iris and my sister, Nell, women who told me the tomb was empty, and for Ruth and Joe Brown Love, who told me my head need not be.

Dedication, James A. Sanders, *God Has a Story, Too*

1. Ken Auletta, "The Lost Tycoon: Now He Has No Wife, No Job, and No Empire, but Ted Turner May Just Save the World," *The New Yorker*, 23 April 2001.

More than two centuries after it destroyed the beautiful buildings of a thriving city, the Lisbon earthquake shattered yet another edifice, this time the once-confident faith of a young biblical scholar named Bart D. Ehrman. It was not the literal shaking of the earth in the Portuguese capital that did the damage, but rather what was symbolized by that dreadful All Saints' Day catastrophe so many generations ago, the shaking of the foundations of trust in a present, powerful, and benevolent God, the crumbling of a comprehensive understanding of life and the world.

In the late 1980s, when Ehrman was thirty years old and an aspiring scholar, the challenge that Lisbon posed for many thoughtful people in the eighteenth century began to be for him a personal, intellectual, and spiritual crisis. Ehrman was then finishing his doctorate in New Testament and serving as the pastor of a small Baptist church, as well as teaching part-time at a nearby university. His university asked him to offer a course called "The Problem of Suffering in the Biblical Traditions," and the questions stirred up by that topic began to ferment in Ehrman's mind until he gradually came to the place where he could no longer believe as he once had done. While the full record of his pilgrimage away from faith is, he says, "a very long story," the crisis that ultimately tipped the balance was the same challenge that Voltaire and other European intellectuals faced after the Lisbon earthquake. Ehrman found himself unable to reconcile faith's picture of a loving and omnipotent God with the realities of innocent suffering in the world. Jesus may have fed the hungry multitudes with bread in the wilderness, but what good is that in a world where a child dies of starvation every five seconds?

In his book describing this loss of faith, *God's Problem: How the Bible Fails to Answer Our Most Important Question — Why We Suffer,* he writes,

> I realized that I could no longer reconcile the claims of faith with the facts of life. In particular, I could no longer explain how there can be a good and all-powerful God actively involved with this world, given the state of things. For many people who inhabit this planet, life is a cesspool of misery and suffering. I came to a point

where I simply could not believe that there is a good and kindly disposed Ruler who is in charge of it.[2]

God's Problem is a significant book, not because it is profound — it is, in fact, theologically somewhat unsophisticated — but because Ehrman expresses the theodicy problem in a street-savvy, commonsense manner recognizable by religiously questing people today, including many who are present in the pews of countless congregations. What tested Ehrman's faith tests the faith of many others today. His language is pitch-perfect; he names the problem of God and innocent suffering, anguishes over it, sifts through the evidence, and evaluates possible responses to the quandary of innocent suffering in just the ways that many other thoughtful people of faith do. Of course, not everyone has traveled with Ehrman to the place where faith has been abandoned, but many share the urgency of his questions and experience the same stresses on their ability to believe. To read *God's Problem* is not only to encounter the views of Bart Ehrman but also to hear the sometimes hidden thoughts and questions of many Christians.

Stalemate

Ehrman was baptized in the Congregational Church and was raised as an Episcopalian, but in his high school days he had a "born again" experience at a Youth for Christ meeting. Ehrman's newfound faith was both fervent and intellectually rigorous. He had been converted to a zealous evangelical faith that rested on the chassis of a brainy, highly logical and rationalistic form of fundamentalism. Not only were Christians devoted to God in their hearts; they were committed in their minds to doctrinal truth claims that they were convinced were unassailably true. In order to nail down any loose planks in his doctrinal system, Ehrman after high school enrolled at Moody Bible Institute in Chicago, which he describes as a "fundamentalist college." After earning a diploma at Moody, he completed his college edu-

2. Bart D. Ehrman, *God's Problem: How the Bible Fails to Answer Our Most Important Question — Why We Suffer* (New York: HarperOne, 2008), p. 3.

cation and reinforced his faith at Wheaton College, a historically evangelical school, which claims Billy Graham as an alumnus.

As Ehrman grew older, however, and gained more education, the tight tethers of his fundamentalism began to fray and finally to break loose. First, there was a crisis over his belief about Scripture. Ehrman learned the inescapable truth that the texts of the Bible, which he had believed were "God-breathed" and infallible, even inerrant, were actually composed by fallible human hands and heavily edited by others. The biblical texts, Ehrman discovered, contained contradictions and discrepancies. What is more, the books that made it into the Bible, into the canon, were there not simply because of inspiration but also because of controversy and political maneuvering. If the Bible was an inspired book, Erhman came to realize, it was inspired in a much messier, much more historically conflicted way than he had imagined. Out went the fundamentalist Bible. And along with it went Ehrman's own fundamentalism.

But not his Christian faith . . . not yet. While problems with the Bible caused him to change his views of Scripture, they did not prompt Ehrman to leave the believing fold. What finally closed the chapel door for Ehrman was not something wrong with the Bible but something wrong, he came to believe, in the God of the Bible. Ehrman simply could not avoid facing the collision between what Scripture claims about the power, presence, and compassion of God and the hard facts of life. The world is full of aching human need and suffering, and as far as Ehrman could see, God seems disinclined to do anything about it:

> The God I once believed in was a God who was active in this world. He saved the Israelites from slavery; he sent Jesus for the salvation of the world; he intervened on behalf of his people when they were in desperate need; he was actively involved in my life. But I can't believe in that God anymore, because from what I now see around the world, he doesn't intervene. One answer to *that* objection is that he intervenes in the hearts of the suffering, bringing them solace and hope in their time of darkest need. It's a nice thought, but I'm afraid that from where I sit, it simply isn't true.[3]

3. Ehrman, *God's Problem*, pp. 15-16.

If Ehrman had lived in the fourteenth century, his sense of injustice about suffering might have provoked him to prayerful lament, to ever-greater cries to heaven for God to come and save. But Ehrman lives on this side of modernity's ditch, and his crisis of faith leads him not to his knees in prayer but to his mind in thinking things through rationally. A fourteenth-century mind would encounter terrible suffering and say, "This is from the hand of God. What is God *saying* to us?" A contemporary mind encounters suffering and asks, "How does the reality of this suffering fit into my worldview? How do the pieces of reality I think of as true fit together logically?" Consequently, as many others since the eighteenth century have done, Ehrman approaches the theological question of God and innocent suffering by setting it up as a logical problem involving the interrelationships among four truth claims that people of faith customarily make:

1. There is a God.
2. God is all-powerful.
3. God is loving and good.
4. There is innocent suffering.[4]

Like many other Christians, Ehrman once saw this list as obvious truths, a set of givens. Of course there is a God, and of course the God

---

4. Ehrman's list contains only three assertions, since he leaves the first one, "There is a God," to be implied. The fourfold statement of the problem is actually a simplification of a more complex philosophical knot. David Ray Griffin expresses the problem in more complete form when he crafts what he calls a "Formal Statement of the Problem of Evil":

    1. God is a perfect reality. (definition)
    2. A perfect reality is an omnipotent being. (by definition)
    3. An omnipotent being could unilaterally bring about an actual world without any evil.
    4. A perfect reality is a morally perfect being. (by definition)
    5. A morally perfect being would want to bring about an actual world without any genuine evil. (by definition)
    6. If there is genuine evil in the world, then there is no God. (logical conclusion from 1 through 5)
    7. There is genuine evil in the world. (factual statement)
    8. Therefore, there is no God. (logical conclusion from 6 and 7)

From David Ray Griffin, *God, Power, and Evil: A Process Theodicy* (Philadelphia: Westminster Press, 1976), p. 9.

who raised Jesus from the dead and defeats the forces of sin and death is all-powerful, and of course the God we see in the face of Jesus is loving and good, and of course there are many occasions in life when people suffer through no apparent fault of their own. All of these assertions are true. However, the problem for Ehrman and many others is that, logically, it does not seem that these claims can be held together as a set. Articulated as direct statements of fact, they clash with each other and cannot all be true at the same time. If God is all-powerful, then God could have kept the Lisbon Cathedral from collapsing onto a congregation of terrified worshipers. If God *could* have done that, would not a truly loving God have chosen to do so?

In John Updike's novel *Rabbit, Run,* a former high-school basketball star named Harry Angstrom is now trapped, as he sees it, in a numbing, dead-end marriage, job, and life. He reacts by engaging in various forms of erratic and irresponsible behavior, including temporarily abandoning his family and moving in with a prostitute. This drives his wife, Janice, into depression and deepening alcoholism. One afternoon, when Harry is absent and Janice is drinking heavily, she attempts to give their infant daughter, Becky, a bath, and the child accidentally drowns in the bathtub. It is Harry and Janice who have been morally questionable; it is the baby who pays the steepest price.

The evening after the accident, Harry returns to their now-empty apartment. He goes into the bathroom, where the water where Becky drowned is still in the tub:

> A heavy, calm volume, odorless, tasteless, colorless, the water shocks him like the presence of a silent person in the bathroom. Stillness makes a dead skin on its unstirred surface. There's even a kind of dust on it. He rolls back his sleeve and reaches down and pulls the plug; the water swings and the drain gasps. He watches the line of water slide slowly and evenly down the wall of the tub, and then with a crazed vortical cry the last of it is sucked away. He thinks how easy it was, yet in all His strength, God did nothing. Just that little rubber stopper to lift.[5]

5. John Updike, *Rabbit, Run* (New York: Ballantine Books, 1960), p. 277.

Just a little rubber stopper to lift. How easy it would have been for an omnipotent God to lift a tiny rubber stopper, and Becky's life would have been spared. If God had the strength to do so, would not a loving God have intervened?

This seeming collision among the four truth claims — there is a God, God is all-powerful, God is good and loving, and there is innocent suffering — has, since the time of Leibniz, constituted the classic formulation of the theodicy problem. Trying to hold on, simultaneously, to these four truth claims can be called "the impossible chess match," a theological stalemate, since no good moves appear available. The eighteenth-century Scottish philosopher David Hume articulated the problem in this memorable way:

> Is [God] willing to prevent evil, but not able? Then he is impotent.
> Is he able, but not willing? Then is he malevolent.
> Is he both able and willing? Whence then is evil?[6]

Faced with the impossible chess match, the only possibility available seems to be to give up one of the truth claims. But which one would we be willing to forfeit? The belief in the existence of God? The goodness of God? The power of God? Or would we close our eyes and deny that there is innocent suffering?

For many in our culture, the notions that God is loving and that God is all-powerful are seen simply as churchly and creedal spins on the more basic claim of theism, that there is a God at all. Thus, these people cut to the chase and view the undeniable reality of overwhelming and innocent suffering in the world as *de facto* evidence against theism. As one Web blogger said, after posting David Hume's quotation on the Internet, "This single quote . . . made me an atheist. What a great quote."[7] Interestingly, this shortcut to atheism may, in fact, be a sign of how deeply biblical understandings of God have settled into Western consciousness. Many secular people do not believe in God, but the God they *don't* believe in is loving, gracious, compassionate, and all-powerful. This effectively reduces

6. David Hume, *Dialogues Concerning Natural Religion,* ed. Martin Bell (London: Penguin, 1991), pp. 108-9. Hume believed that he was quoting the Greek philosopher Epicurus, but the source of this statement in Epicurus is obscure.

7. See http://en.wikiquote.org/wiki/Talk:Epicurus.

the impossible chess match to two positions: claim one, there is a God who is loving, compassionate, and powerful; and claim two, there is innocent suffering. Since two is clearly true, one, as a whole package, has to be jettisoned.

As for Ehrman, he equivocates some, but he finally seems inclined toward the same choice: "I don't 'know' if there is a God," he says, "but I think that if there is one, he certainly isn't the one proclaimed by the Judeo-Christian tradition, the one who is actively and powerfully involved in this world. And so I stopped going to church."[8]

Missing God

Whatever sadness I may feel about Bart Ehrman as a person of lost faith, I remain grateful to him for the way he states the theodicy problem. He talks and reasons in the direct, no-nonsense way that corresponds to that of many thinking Christians, and he makes it clear, I think, how high are the stakes. The inescapable logic of "the impossible chess match" leads many faithful people inevitably toward the very same last move as Ehrman's, the abandonment of one's confidence in God. Many of the best and brightest Christians are trying to thrash their way through the thicket of the theodicy problem, and they are using the same tools and resources as Ehrman does. The fact that, like Ehrman, they are having a difficult time finding a clear way through should be of great concern to those who preach.

As I hope to show in the later pages of this book, I think it takes theological imagination to find our way through these questions faithfully. I believe it is precisely theological imagination that Ehrman lacks, and it finally costs him in the end. He is no longer a fundamentalist, but in many ways he still thinks like one, unable to escape the stiffness of its categories and woodenness of its rationalist logic. But in the way he poses the problem, he is a reliable guide. He quite rightly will not accept sentimental piety for hard truth. He refuses mere poetry as a substitute for clear logic.

8. Ehrman, *God's Problem*, p. 125.

We preach today not to the cherubim and the seraphim but to people many of whom belong to the secular world at least as firmly as they belong to the church, people who have one foot in the faith, perhaps, but who firmly plant the other foot in a world of science and reason. If we ask them to believe the gospel, the gospel must, in some way, "make sense" to them. This does not mean whittling down the gospel to fit the categories of modern, rational science. To the contrary, it means, at times, challenging those very categories, attempting to expand the possibilities of what can "make sense" to people and what can be received by them as true. Ehrman's filters on truth are set by historicism and literalism, and they are finally too narrow. The biggest and deepest truths ultimately cannot pass through to him. But when he says, in effect, "Hey, you claim that God is loving and that God is powerful, but when a little girl walking home with a handful of flowers for her mother is hit and killed by a drunk driver and God didn't stop it from happening, you have some explaining to do," he not only speaks for many, but he is right to say it.

But what is also valuable about Ehrman's book is how touchingly he exposes his hunger for something more than his plucky skepticism. He tries to come across as the tough-minded, brave, intellectual agnostic, too smart, too honest, and too committed to the unvarnished truth to be swayed any longer by the superstitions of naïve Christianity. But he is actually closer to British novelist Julian Barnes, who begins his memoirs with this sentence: "I don't believe in God, but I miss Him."[9]

Ehrman misses God. I think he wants to be preached to in a way that doesn't insult his intelligence but that also opens him up once again to the experience of God. At one point he says that part of the pain of being an unbeliever is that, in his words,

> I have such a fantastic life that I feel an overwhelming sense of gratitude for it; I am fortunate beyond words. But I don't have anyone to express my gratitude to. This is a void deep inside me, a void of wanting someone to thank, and I don't see any plausible way of filling it.[10]

9. Julian Barnes, *Nothing to Be Frightened Of* (New York: Alfred A. Knopf, 2008), p. 3.
10. Ehrman, *God's Problem*, p. 128.

But even deeper than this wistfulness about thanksgiving is what seems to be, at times, Ehrman's puzzlingly ardent defense of the sovereignty of God, the sovereignty of the God he is not sure exists. At one point in the book he is discussing the view, advanced by a number of Christian theologians, that the key to understanding the gospel's response to the theodicy problem is in the very suffering of God in Christ. Ehrman rejects this view as too soft. A suffering God? Such a notion, Ehrman complains, sacrifices "the view that God is sovereign over his creation . . . God is not really GOD"[11] — an odd objection for an agnostic to make.

Ehrman even seems enraged at God's failure to be GOD. He reports that he went to a Christmas Eve service one year because his wife, who is a believer, asked him to go with her. Ehrman found the service emotionally disturbing, especially the congregational prayer, which consisted of a layperson standing in the midst of the congregation praying, "You came into the darkness and made a difference. Come into the darkness again." This prayer, Ehrman says, brought him to tears, but not tears of joy — tears of frustration. "Why *doesn't* [God] enter into the darkness again?" he wonders. "Where is the presence of God in this world of pain and misery? Why is the darkness so overwhelming?"[12] In other words, I don't know if you exist, God, but "O that you would rend the heavens and come down."

Ehrman is perhaps a more radicalized version of many church-going Christians. In this kind of world, the gospel of the good and all-powerful God in control of the events of this world does not ring entirely true, but he keeps going into the morgue where the lifeless body of the late, lamented God lies in state and shouting, "Are you still dead, God? Please don't be dead. I don't believe in you, but I miss you."

In his magisterial and brilliant book on secularity, *A Secular Age*, philosopher and Catholic layman Charles Taylor describes this kind of anguish, Ehrman's anguish, the anguish of some of the most thoughtful people in our churches, the anguish of people who are caught between a faith that they can't fully accept intellectually and a secularity they can't

11. Ehrman, *God's Problem*, p. 274.
12. Ehrman, *God's Problem*, p. 5.

accept spiritually. Taylor says that much of the secularism in our culture is not the result of religious devotion slipping away but of the rise of alternative ways to describe reality that seem to have more persuasive power than the language of faith. Taylor writes:

> Today, when a naturalistic materialism is not only an offer, but presents itself as the only view compatible with the most prestigious situation of the modern world, viz., science; it is quite conceivable that one's doubts about one's own faith, about one's ability to be transformed, or one's sense of how one's own faith is childish and inadequate, could mesh with this powerful ideology, and send one off along the path of unbelief, even though with regret and nostalgia.[13]

One could hardly state the challenge to preaching today more aptly. There they are out there in the pews, people who want to believe but who are plagued by honest doubts, people who are reminded every day in ways explicit and implicit that their faith in a God who loves humanity and acts in the world benevolently is merely the "unresolved residue of childish fantasy," people who are pressed by the powerful ideology of science and the pressure of a secular culture to pack their intellectual bags and to head out "East of Eden" along the road of unbelief, but who leave reluctantly and with regret and nostalgia, looking back as they go to see if someone, anyone, will speak a word that kindles their faith once again and gives them hope that God is alive and that life is more than a flat, technological world ruled by raw human ambition and power and punctuated by random and meaningless suffering.

A Ministry of Presence?

Most seminary-trained pastors are aware, of course, of the theodicy problem. Bart Ehrman is by no means the first, nor will he be the last, to articulate it. We know that for centuries philosophers and theologians have been wrestling through the question of God and innocent suffering,

13. Charles Taylor, *A Secular Age* (Cambridge: Belknap Press, 2007), p. 28.

but as pastors we have been warned to steer well clear of the theodicy problem. Pastors today have been firmly taught that the question is impossible; we cannot explain suffering and evil, we cannot justify the ways of God, and, when we are in the pastoral role, attempting to do so can do far more harm than good. When we are caring for a woman whose husband has just died of a sudden and massive heart attack, leaving her with two small children, an unpaid mortgage, and an uncertain future, we do well to grieve with her, to stand supportively with her, but to keep our mouths shut about what we think all this tragedy may mean. To offer any reason for what happened or to speculate about God's role in it beyond an affirmation that "God is with you in your suffering" is to trivialize her experience and to try to explain it away. When we are asked what we have to offer, what the gospel has to offer, in such a crisis, we sometimes respond that we have a "ministry of presence." Except for words of consolation and solidarity, no words at all, just compassionate presence.

I do not wish to challenge the ministry of presence as an approach to pastoral care in times of grief. Sometimes just being there with people in a time of need speaks volumes, and the last thing we need are pastors who, like Job's friends, are full of chatty and superficial explanations for people's suffering. But I do wish to challenge the image of a "ministry of presence" as a comprehensive approach to the questions of evil and suffering. Times of deep and raw grief may not be the best teachable moments, but there *are* teachable moments. For many Christians, the question of suffering, theirs and others, is not just a pastoral care matter; it is an intellectually troubling issue, one that they think about a great deal but do not have the resources to think through. They want to love God with their minds as well as their hearts, but they can't see their way clear. Just because pastors do not have a magic bullet, an "Aha!" answer to the problem of suffering that will make it all plain, does not mean that we do not have a long history of ways of thinking this issue through. Done most faithfully, pondering the question of suffering and the love of God is a form of prayer, and I think preachers owe congregations the benefits of this intellectual questing, this form of prayer in which faith seeks understanding.

What is at stake here, first, is the very basis of faith, the claim that life is rich with the mystery of God. When Diane Komp, a pediatric cancer specialist now retired from Yale Medical School, was a young physician, she

considered herself to be a "post-Christian doctor," a scientist who "vacil-
lated between being an agnostic and an atheist" and who cared little about
where she fell on that scale at any given moment.[14] Her medical specialty
called for her to care for children with cancer, some of them terminal. The
first time she faced such a case, a child who was dying, she asked her clini-
cal mentor how she, as a young doctor, should handle the emotional stress
of encountering innocent suffering. The response was that she should for-
get her feelings and concentrate on her work. "Hard work," her mentor
said, "is a good tonic for untamed and uneasy feelings."[15]

Komp quickly discovered the impossibility of this counsel. To treat
her children patients effectively, she had to listen attentively to them,
and to their parents, and to do that meant, over time, that she came to
love them and to receive love from them. It also meant realizing that
these children and their parents were struggling with far more than a bi-
ological disease. They were wrestling with questions about the meaning
of suffering, life, and death. So Komp was caught in the same dilemma
facing many pastors: she could not maintain an emotional detachment
because she loved her patients and their families, but she had little to offer them in response to their non-medical questions of meaning. So, she
decided to assume with her patients something akin to what clergy
would call "a ministry of presence":

> . . . I did not pretend to have any handy theological solutions to
> people's existential dilemmas, but I could be a friend on the way.
> Many times I listened politely to parents who groped for God in
> their most painful hour. I respected them all for their journeys,
> but I heard no convincing evidence in their revelations to chal-
> lenge my way of thinking. If I were to believe, I always assumed, it
> would require the testimony of reliable witnesses. . . .[16]

But then Komp found herself at the bedside of Anna. Anna became
sick with leukemia when she was two. In the next few years, she received

---

14. Diane Komp, *A Window to Heaven: When Children See Life in Death* (Grand
Rapids: Zondervan, 1992), p. 22.
15. Komp, *A Window to Heaven*, p. 23.
16. Komp, *A Window to Heaven*, p. 27.

constant therapy, and there were times when she was disease-free. But at age seven, the leukemia had returned with an unforgiving vengeance, and this time Anna was facing the end. Komp gathered with Anna's distraught parents and a hospital chaplain to comfort Anna in her last few minutes of life. She describes what happened:

> Before she died, [Anna] mustered the final energy to sit up in her hospital bed and say, "The angels — they're so beautiful. Do you hear their singing? I've never heard such beautiful singing!" Then she laid back on her pillow and died.
>
> Her parents reacted as if they had been given the most precious gift in the world. The hospital chaplain in attendance was more comfortable with the psychological than with the spiritual, and he beat a hasty retreat to leave the existentialist doctor alone with the grieving family. Together we contemplated a spiritual mystery that transcended our understanding and experience. For weeks to follow, the thought that stuck in my head was: Have I found a reliable witness?[17]

Notice two things about this experience. The first is the sad truth of the chaplain "more comfortable with the psychological than with the spiritual," who makes a quick exit from a room suddenly filled with mystery. When pastors themselves capitulate to a ministry of the manageable, a prayer book of only empirical explanations, small wonder that their parishioners feel overwhelmed in a secular age. The second is that the "existentialist doctor," now wondering if she had found at last a reliable witness, stepped into the proper pastoral role, moving beyond a ministry of silent presence to join with a family in contemplating "a spiritual mystery that transcended our understanding and experience." People sense that there is more at hand than the measurable, quantifiable facts, and this is not mere wishful thinking. They are, to use Komp's words, "groping for God in their most painful hour," and good pastors do not stand there mute. We have a legacy of centuries of courageous Christian thinkers who have thought their way through the toughest questions life can pose. We obviously don't want to turn a hospital bedside, or

---

17. Komp, *A Window to Heaven*, pp. 28-29.

a sanctuary, into a seminar room, and we should be humble in the light of mysteries too deep for words, but to stand there silently, as if all the gospel has to offer in the face of suffering is our little presence, is to deprive the faithful of their own theological inheritance.

What is at stake here is not only the very basis of faith but also our ability to worship authentically. Several years ago, I had lunch with a dear friend, a pastor in a richly liturgical tradition who, as a part of our table conversation, teased me, saying, "I don't understand you Presbyterians. You are so cussedly theological, always trying to get your doctrines right, always fighting over theology. In my church, we step around the doctrinal fussing and feuding and just meet God in the liturgy, in the prayers and at the table." A few weeks later, however, my friend sent me an e-mail in which she said, "I have been thinking some more about this whole issue of doctrine and theology, and I've been having a few new thoughts. Sometimes the problem in my tradition is that we are stuck with this ancient liturgy that needs SO MUCH HELP before some of us can say it. We recite traditional atonement theory every Sunday; we say the old creed. If you don't have a way of understanding this language in fresh and relevant ways, you finally can't speak it with integrity."

What I hear in this exchange is not a preference for one ecclesial tradition over another (I am often ashamed over the bitter theological battles, so devoid of charity, that regularly break out like fistfights at hockey games in my own tradition), but a recognition that there is a necessary and fruitful relationship between the ancient liturgy of the church and an ongoing, creative theological rethinking of the language of worship. The language of worship is poetry, and sometimes that poetry needs to be altered or even abandoned. The metaphors of even good poetry can go stale or become impossibly remote in new settings.[18] Most of the

18. As an example of liturgical metaphors becoming impossibly remote, one could hardly do better than to cite, along with hymnologist Brian Wren, Charles Wesley's 1742 hymn stanza "To me, to all, thy bowels move; Thy nature, and thy name is love." In the eighteenth century, to "move one's bowels" was equivalent to what we mean by "to respond with deep emotion." By the late nineteenth century, though, "move bowels" language had shifted to refer to ordinary bodily function. Even the most loyal Wesleyans had to recognize that some metaphors are best abandoned and so changed Charles's hymn to read "To me, to all, thy mercies move; Thy nature, and thy name is love." See

time, however, the time-tested metaphors of our hymns and prayers retain their value, but only in the context of theological re-imagining. Let's say we're going to ask people to sing this:

> Praise to the Lord, Who o'er all things so wondrously reigneth,
> Shelters thee under His wings, yea, so gently sustaineth!
> Hast thou not seen
> How thy desires e'er have been
> Granted in what He ordaineth?

Thinking people are going to need a way to interpret and understand and own that language. Is it possible and desirable to say that God "so wondrously reigneth"? I believe the answer is yes, but only if "so wondrously reigneth" does not also imply a God who summons tsunamis from the sea to drown thousands of terrified people begging for mercy.

If our basic belief in God as well as our capacity to pray and to sing and to worship are at stake in moving beyond a ministry of presence, I also think that a third concern is on the table: the understanding of the Christian faith as the affirmation of a God involved in human history. The inability to make some kind of sense of the actions and will of God in a world of suffering and evil puts pressure on people of faith — sometimes subtle, sometimes not-so-subtle — to abandon the biblical claim that God is a God of history, of time, of material embodiment and actual circumstances, in favor of a mystical God of nature and spirituality. If people in our day are "spiritual but not religious," could it be that this is not simply because they are individualistic narcissists or people who find "institutional religion" bland and confining, but because they have lost a meaningful way to speak and think about a God who acts in history, in institutions, in actual human relationships, in concrete circumstances.

In his powerful book *After Auschwitz*, the Jewish theologian Richard L. Rubenstein describes how, for him and others, the catastrophic suffering of the *Shoah* first cut them off from the worship of the synagogue, and then from the God of history. It began as silence in the house of prayer:

Brian Wren, *Praying Twice: The Music and Words of Congregational Song* (Louisville: Westminster John Knox Press, 2000), p. 297.

34

For those of us who lived through the terrible years, whether in safety or as victims, the *Shoah* conditions the way we encounter all things sacred and profane. Nothing in our experience is untouched by that absolutely decisive event. Because of the *Shoah*, some of us enter the synagogue to partake of our sacred times and seasons with those to whom we are bound in shared memory, pain, fate, and hope; yet, once inside, we are struck dumb by words we can no longer honestly utter. All that we can offer is our reverent and attentive silence before the Divine.[19]

The "attentive silence before the Divine" gradually becomes attention to a different sort of divine presence, a form of nature spirituality:

After Auschwitz and the return to Israel, the God of Nature, or more precisely the God who manifests Himself, so to speak, in and through nature, was the God to whom the Jews would turn in place of the God of History, especially in Israel. . . . My rejection of the biblical God of History led me to a modified form of nature paganism.[20]

These reasons to move beyond a ministry of presence are made all the more compelling because they take the form of cries from people of faith for their pastors to give them more than we often give them. The problem of God's presence and role among innocent sufferers is not an abstract conundrum, a theological parlor game. Every day people in congregations face suffering for which their theology is not sufficient. As a moving example of this, consider the theologian Lewis Smedes's account of his own experience with suffering. Early in their marriage, Smedes and his wife, Doris, were trying in vain to conceive a child. Smedes writes,

We had spent a decade making love according to a schedule set by four different fertility clinics in three different countries. And finally, after one summer night's lark on the sand dunes of Lake Michigan with no thought but love, Doris became a medically certified pregnant woman.

19. Richard L. Rubenstein, *After Auschwitz: History, Theology, and Contemporary Judaism,* 2d ed. (Baltimore: Johns Hopkins Press, 1992), p. 200.
20. Rubenstein, *After Auschwitz,* p. 175.

Six months along and doing fine, we thought — with God answering our prayers it could be no other way but fine — she suddenly one night began losing amniotic fluid. I called her doctor. "She's going into labor," he said. "Get her to the hospital as fast as you can." And then he said he was sorry, but our baby was going to be badly malformed.

"How badly?"

"Very."

We fumbled silent and bewildered into the car. I told her. We cried. And we promised God and each other that we would love the child no matter how damaged she or he was. After Doris had been tucked in, I went to the waiting room to worry for a few hours. Suddenly, Doris's doctor broke in and exulted: "Congratulations, Lew, you are the father of a perfect man-child." I told Doris the news. She was skeptical, but I went home and danced like a delirious David before the Lord.

Next day, just before noon, our pediatrician called: I had better come right down to the hospital. When I met him he told me that our miracle child was dead. Two mornings later, with a couple of friends at my side and our minister reading the ceremony, we buried him "in the sure and certain hope of the resurrection." Doris never got to see her child.

A pious neighbor comforted me by reminding me that "God was in control." I wanted to say to her, "Not this time."

. . . I had been intellectually excited by John Calvin's tough-minded belief that all things — and he really meant all of them, including the ghastly and the horrible — happen when and how and where they happen precisely as God decreed them to happen. A "horrific decree," Calvin conceded, but if it works out to God's glory, who are we to complain? On the day that our baby boy died, I knew that I could never again believe that God had arranged for our tiny child to die before he had hardly begun to live, any more than I could believe that we would, one fine day when he would make it all plain, praise God that it had happened.

. . . I do not want God to "make it plain." If God could show us that there was a good and necessary reason for such a bad thing

36

to have happened, it must not have been a bad thing after all. And I cannot accommodate that thought.

I learned that I do not have the right stuff for such hard-boiled theology. I am no more able to believe that God micro-manages the death of little children than I am able to believe that God was macro-managing Hitler's Holocaust. With one morning's wrenching intuition, I knew that my portrait of God would have to be repainted.[21]

How many of our people are repainting their portrait of God, but without the help of the Christian thinkers and theologians who have walked this path before them? There are some theologians who say that we should not venture onto this territory at all, that the so-called theodicy problem — in the way that Bart Ehrman and others frame it — is so badly mangled by philosophers that theology should politely excuse it-self from the conversation. We will explore their objections later. But, no matter what their objections are, there is a sense in which preachers do not have the option of fully heeding them. If people are asking the theodicy question in approximately the terms used by Ehrman, we preachers cannot simply scream, "Foul ball! Illegitimate theological question!" Even if their questions are framed all wrong, they are their questions, and they are the questions with which we must begin.

I agree with Christian philosopher Marilyn McCord Adams, who says that people who experience trauma and horrors eventually get around to asking questions of meaning, and they raise them in language not much different from that of Bart Ehrman or Ted Turner, whose own loss of faith was described at the opening of this chapter. They raise the familiar questions: Did God allow this? Why? Can God redeem this? Is there reason to go on? Adams says,

> They demand of us, their friends and counselors, not only that we sit *shivah* with them, but also that we help them try to make sense of their experience. They look to us for hints, beg for coaching as they embrace, struggle to sustain the spiritually difficult assign-

21. Lewis B. Smedes, "What's God Up To?: A Father Grieves the Loss of a Child," *Christian Century*, 3 May 2003, p. 38.

ment of integrating their experiences of the Goodness of God and horrendous evil into the whole of a meaningful life.[22]

Adams says this came home to her most forcefully when she was working at a California church during the rise of the HIV/AIDS epidemic. "Spiritually desperate gays and lesbians," people who would have described themselves as "church damaged" by their experiences of rejection for their sexuality, nevertheless starting coming back to church. Now in their thirties and forties, they were facing death, in themselves and their partners, and they came back to the church with urgent questions: What did the God they remembered from their childhood have to do with this deadly plague? What did it have to do with their being gay or lesbian?[23]

> Sunday mornings, when I looked out on the congregation, into their faces, gray-green from doses of AZT, I could feel their demand: "It's now or never. We'll be dead in six weeks. For God's sake, think of a way to show us how — despite this present ruin — God loves us. Isn't there, surely there must be, a good word for us from the Lord?"[24]

That is the situation for all of us. We are always facing death. The time is urgent. For God's sake, talk to us. Does God love us? Show us how. Is there a good word from the Lord? Speak to us.

When I was in my first year as a parish minister, a disaster happened in another church. At 11:28 on a crisp October Sunday morning, while my congregation was in worship and singing "Fairest Lord Jesus," the boiler exploded in the First Baptist Church in Marietta, Ohio. There were 140 people in the building at the time, some of them in Sunday school, others in the sanctuary listening to organ music. Five of them died — a thirty-year-old Sunday school teacher, married and the father of a child, and four teenagers who were in his class. They were in a classroom directly beneath the boiler room. Fourteen others in the building were injured.

---

22. Marilyn McCord Adams, *Horrendous Evils and the Goodness of God* (Ithaca, N.Y.: Cornell University Press, 1999), p. 188.

23. Marilyn McCord Adams, "Afterword," in *Encountering Evil: Live Options in Theodicy*, ed. Stephen T. Davis (Louisville: Westminster John Knox Press, 2001), p. 191.

24. Adams, "Afterword," p. 192.

The next Sunday at my church, a group of my parishioners and I were talking about this incident, how inexplicable it was that innocent children and their Sunday school teacher had their lives extinguished in a moment of pain. I said to the group, "Well, I'll tell you one thing. I would hate to have to make sense of that. I'm glad I am not the pastor of that church."

One of the group looked straight at me. "You are the pastor of that church," she said.

And so are we all.

In the next chapter, then, we will begin to explore what the Christian tradition can help us say, what the gospel can help us say, to help people find meaning in the midst of a world of innocent suffering.

CHAPTER THREE

Road Hazards

~*~

The illiterate peasant who comments on the death of a child by referring to the will of God is engaging in theodicy as much as the learned theologian who writes a treatise to demonstrate that the suffering of the innocent does not negate the conception of a God both all-good and all-powerful.

Peter Berger, *The Sacred Canopy*[1]

Preachers who want to reflect deeply on the question of God's goodness and power in relation to innocent suffering in the world — that is, on the theodicy question — are not without companionship. Many thoughtful people of faith, especially over the last two centuries, have pondered these issues. Beginning in the next chapter, we will travel down the pilgrim road with some of the best of these thinkers, learning what we can and challenging what we must. As we go, however, there are two important warning signs along the highway that we must heed.

1. Peter Berger, *The Sacred Canopy: Elements of a Sociological Theory of Religion* (New York: Anchor Books, 1969), p. 53.

Speaking the Truth, Speaking in Love

The first warning comes in the form of an ethical question posed by theologian David Bentley Hart in his book *The Doors of the Sea: Where Was God in the Tsunami?* He cites a *New York Times* article published shortly after the devastation of the Indian Ocean tsunami.[2] The article brought the enormity of this tragedy down to a very human scale by telling the story of a Sri Lankan father, a large man of great physical strength, who, despite desperate efforts, including trying to swim through the boiling sea with the arms of his wife and mother-in-law wrapped around his neck, was nevertheless unable to prevent any of his four children or his wife from being swept to their deaths by the surging waters. As he told the reporter the names of his lost children, in descending order by age, ending with the name of his four-year-old son, the father was utterly overcome with deep sobbing and grief and disbelief. "My wife and children must have thought, 'Father is here . . . he will save us,' he said, crying. 'I couldn't do it.'"

Here's the ethical dilemma: If one had the opportunity to speak to this man at the very moment of his tears, at his most fragile time of grief, what should one say? Not what *could* be said, but what *should* be said? According to Hart, only a "moral cretin" would have approached the father at that moment with some abstract theological explanation: "Sir, your children's deaths are a part of God's eternal but mysterious counsels," or "Your children's deaths, tragic as they may seem, in the larger sense serve God's complex design for creation."[3]

"Most of us," says Hart, "would have the good sense to be ashamed to speak such words" to this broken father.[4] Hart goes on to turn this test into a rule: "And this should tell us something. For if we think it shamefully foolish and cruel to say such things in the moment when another's sorrow is most real and irresistibly painful, then *we ought never to say them*."[5]

2. Amy Waldman, "Torn from Moorings, Villagers from Sri Lanka Grasp for Past," *The New York Times*, 6 March 2005.

3. David Bentley Hart, *The Doors of the Sea: Where Was God in the Tsunami?* (Grand Rapids: Wm. B. Eerdmans, 2005), pp. 99-100.

4. Hart, *The Doors of the Sea*, p. 100.

5. Hart, *The Doors of the Sea*, p. 100, emphasis added.

This is a good rule, I believe, for preaching on the theodicy question. If we think we have some insight or wisdom about the theodicy problem, about God, evil, and suffering, but it is not a word that we would want to speak to a sufferer in the depths of loss and grief, then this is a trustworthy sign that this so-called "wisdom" is not really the gospel, and it should not be spoken at all.

Theologian Terrence Tilley shares Hart's contempt for all abstract "solutions" to the theodicy problem that run roughshod over real suffering. Tilley singles out for particular scorn Cardinal Charles Journet's classic work of Thomist theology, *The Meaning of Evil,* in which Journet turns away from the actual cries of suffering people to address the issue in its purer form, what he calls "the metaphysical difficulty."[6] Journet ends his book by reassuring his readers that "if ever evil, at any time in history, should threaten to surpass the good, God would annihilate the world and all its workings."[7] These are, Tilley says sarcastically, "truly comforting final words." Can you imagine saying this to the Sri Lankan father? "That was a tough loss you took, sir, but I can assure you that should evil ever really get out of hand, God will bring this entire earth experiment to a halt." Tilley is repulsed. "At [Journet's] high level of abstraction, not only are practical concerns which generate problems for religious believers ignored, but so marginalized and distorted that the possibility of God's destruction of the whole world God created is rendered a good thing!"[8]

One small amendment, possibly, needs to be made to Hart's ethical rule. What Hart, quite rightly, is trying to eliminate from our theological repertoire are those responses to the theodicy problem that are perhaps satisfying at some abstract level but become cruel mockeries when placed into the context of actual human suffering. What Hart opposes is a posture of cold detachment, like that taken by one theologian who said of the theodicy issue, "The practical problem is pastoral, medical, or psychological, and differs from case to case too widely to allow of much useful generalization. We are concerned with the theoretical problem only.

6. Terrence W. Tilley, *The Evils of Theodicy* (Eugene, Ore.: Wipf & Stock, 2000), p. 229.

7. Charles Journet, *The Meaning of Evil* (New York: P. J. Kennedy & Sons, 1963), p. 289.

8. Tilley, *The Evils of Theodicy,* p. 230.

If what we say is neither comforting nor tactful, we need not mind. Our business is to say, if we can, what is true."[9] Kenneth Surin is equally strong when he says, "To regard theodicy as a purely theoretical and scholarly exercise is to provide — albeit unwillingly — a tacit sanction of the myriad evils that exist on this planet."[10] To say to the Sri Lankan father that the death of his wife and four children fits into some theoretical understanding of theodicy would imply a cold and distant God, or even a God who is a moral monster. It would not only lack comfort and tact; it would not be the gospel truth.

A very different matter, though, is the question of timing in speaking pastoral truth. Some aspects of the gospel await the proper moment to be spoken. For example, William Sloane Coffin said in his famous sermon preached shortly after the death of his son Alex that he had received a "healing flood of letters" from many people, but he went on to say that not all of these words of comfort were genuinely comforting:

> Some of the very best, and easily the worst, came from fellow reverends, a few of whom proved they knew their Bibles better than the human condition. I know all the "right" biblical passages, including "Blessed are those who mourn," and my faith is no house of cards; these passages are true, I know. But the point is this. While the words of the Bible are true, grief renders them unreal. The reality of grief is the absence of God — "My God, my God, why hast thou forsaken me?"[11]

Because of the rawness and depth of Coffin's grief, the "right" biblical passages could at first be heard only as "unreal." But it is significant that this changed for Coffin as time passed. Later in the sermon, he observes that "as the grief that once seemed unbearable begins to turn now to bearable sorrow, the truths in the 'right' biblical passages are beginning, once again, to take hold. . . ."[12] In other words, while we want to say noth-

9. Austin Farrer, *Love Almighty and Ills Unlimited* (London: Fontana Books, 1966), p. 7.

10. Kenneth Surin, *Theology and the Problem of Evil* (Oxford: Basil Blackwell, 1986), p. 50.

11. William Sloane Coffin, "Alex's Death," *The Collected Sermons of William Sloane Coffin: The Riverside Years*, vol. 2 (Philadelphia: Westminster John Knox, 2008), p. 4.

12. Coffin, "Alex's Death."

ing at any time to anyone that we could not say to a person in deep grief, there is a pastoral wisdom in finding the right time to speak certain truths. When people are in the midst of trauma, even when they turn to us to ask "why?" this is usually not the time to think carefully and theologically through the problem of suffering, but there is a time to work through the problem, so that people can love God with their minds as well as with their hearts.

What God? Whose Understanding?

The second warning that is given as we set out on an exploration of responses to the theodicy question is more complex and perhaps more stern. Some theologians are persuaded, quite frankly, that we are on a fool's mission. An expedition into the region of theodicy, they believe, will be futile, at best, and theologically dangerous, at worst.

In order to understand why this warning is sounded, we need to go back to Lisbon in 1755 and back to the origins of what has come to be called "theodicy." At that point in history, European philosophers and scientists not only possessed a growing admiration for the powers of science and reason to describe the universe; they also felt an increasing disgust over the dogmatism and narrowness of the churches, both Protestant and Catholic. Small wonder. Europe had been devastated and morally exhausted by religious warfare. The public face of religion was often authoritarian, repressive, violent, and socially domineering, all in the name of "true religion." Moreover, in an age when individualism, reason, and autonomy were in intellectual vogue, nothing could seem more petty, irrelevant, and perhaps even dangerous than the churches' intramural disputes over matters like predestination and human depravity, doctrines that seemed to diminish the freedom and dignity of the individual.

In many ways, the place of religion in eighteenth-century culture bears resemblances to the place of religion in our own time. Much of the world's violence today seems to spring from religious conflict and intolerance. The voices of rigid dogmatism scream the loudest. The intellectual class in Europe in the eighteeenth century was sick of sectarianism, weary of religious violence, and inclined to reject any theological views

45

made on the basis of churchly authority alone. The question was no longer what do the Scriptures or the pope or the creeds say, but, as Jeffrey Stout has named it, "What might be said in favor of God's existence if we do not assume from the beginning that certain documents and persons possess divine authority?"[13] Some of the more outspoken of these philosophers were not unlike today's "new atheists," writing books full of confidence in science and reason and scorn for religion's violent and superstitious tendencies. When Christopher Hitchens, in *God Is Not Great: How Religion Poisons Everything*, scolds religion for being intellectually closed and intolerant, he writes in the twenty-first century, but his views find their roots in the eighteenth century:

> It can be stated as a truth that religion does not, and in the long run cannot, be content with its own marvelous claims and sublime assurances. It *must* seek to interfere with the lives of unbelievers, or heretics, or adherents of other faiths. It may speak about the bliss of the next world, but it wants power in this one. This is only to be expected. It is, after all, wholly man-made. And it does not have the confidence in its own various preachings even to allow coexistence between different faiths.[14]

One major difference between Hitchens, or Richard Dawkins, in our time and the Enlightenment philosophers is that, for the most part, the eighteenth-century intellectuals did not turn from conventional religion to atheism. A few did, but most Enlightenment intellectuals desired to maintain a belief in God, just not the narrowly defined, irrational "gods" of the sects. To use language from our time, they wanted to be "spiritual, but not religious," if "spiritual" meant clearheaded belief in a God whose nature made sense to reason and if "religious" meant blind and ignorant allegiance to the hopelessly compromised kind of deity worshiped by the Lutherans or the Calvinists or the Catholics.

These philosophical views of religion came shipboard across the At-

---

13. Jeffrey Stout, *The Flight from Authority: Religion, Morality, and the Quest for Autonomy* (Notre Dame: University of Notre Dame Press, 1981), p. 169.

14. Christopher Hitchens, *God Is Not Great: How Religion Poisons Everything* (New York: Twelve Books, 2007), p. 17.

lantic to the colonies, and some of the more philosophically astute of the American founders shared their European counterparts' distaste for the older revealed religions and a preference for the God disclosed in nature and to human reason. Thomas Paine, for example, wrote, in language worthy of Dawkins and Hitchens,

> The most detestable wickedness, the most horrid cruelties, and the greatest miseries that have afflicted the human race, have had their origin in this thing called revelation, or revealed religion. It has been the most dishonourable belief against the character of the divinity, the most destructive to morality and the peace and happiness of man, that ever was propagated since man began to exist. It is better, far better, that we admitted, if it were possible, a thousand devils to roam at large, and to preach publicly the doctrine of devils, if there were any such, than that we permitted one such impostor and monster as Moses, Joshua, Samuel, and the Bible prophets, to come with the pretended word of God in his mouth, and have credit among us.[15]

John Adams, a former Congregationalist whose philosophical views coaxed him to Unitarianism, wrote in a letter to his Deist friend, Thomas Jefferson, of the defects of Trinitarian creedalism and the virtues of natural religion:

> The human Understanding is a revelation from its Maker which can never be disputed or doubted. . . . No Prophecies, no Miracles are necessary to prove this celestial communication. This revelation has made it certain that two and one make three; and that one is not three; nor can three be one. We can never be so certain of any Prophecy, or the fulfillment of any Prophecy; or of any miracle, or the design of any miracle as We are, from the revelation of nature . . . that two and two are equal to four. . . . Howl, snarl, bite, Ye Calvinistick! Ye Athanasian Divines, if You will. Ye will say, I am

---

15. Paine, *The Age of Reason,* quoted in *A Documentary History of Religion in America to 1877,* ed. Edwin S. Gaustad and Mark A. Noll 3rd ed. (Grand Rapids: Wm. B. Eerdmans, 2003), p. 268.

no Christian; I say Ye are no Christians; and there the Account is ballanced.[16]

Jefferson, in a letter in response to Adams, agreed:

If, by *religion,* we are to understand *Sectarian dogmas* . . . then your exclamation on that hypothesis is just, "that this would be the best of all possible worlds, if there were no religion in it." But if the moral precepts, innate in man, and made a part of his physical constitution, as necessary for a social being, if the sublime doctrines of philanthropism, and deism taught us by Jesus of Nazareth in which all agree, constitute true religion, then, without it, this would be, as you again say, "something not fit to be named, even indeed a Hell."[17]

Note that Jefferson sharply contrasts "sectarian dogmas" with the "true religion" of an inward morality and a deistic theology, and that he puts Jesus of Nazareth on his side. Enlightenment thinkers were busy replacing the churchly God — the God of the Bible, of history, of story, of creed, and of Trinitarian confession — with a kinder and gentler deity, the God whose majesty was radiant in nature and whose character was universally accessible to human reason and reflection. This was a God who, to their minds, did not have bloody hands, a God who needed no logic-fracturing Trinitarian formulas to be described and understood, a God who was content to preside over the ordered cosmos and who did not insist on making axe heads float, turning water into wine, or committing any other credulity-shattering miraculous violations of natural law. This was a God fully compatible with the Newtonian conception of the universe, a God who was the Grand Architect of the natural order and whose role was to watch over and preserve the master design. For many of the Enlightenment philosophers, the choice was clear: on the one hand, they could no longer accept the "superstitions" of orthodox Christianity, but, on the other hand, they could not contemplate becom-

16. Letter from John Adams to Thomas Jefferson, Sept. 14, 1813, in *A Documentary History of Religion in America to 1877,* pp. 260-70.

17. Letter from Thomas Jefferson to John Adams, May 5, 1817, in *A Documentary History of Religion in America to 1877,* pp. 270-71.

ing atheists, either; so they became Deists or pantheists or transcendental spiritualists.[18]

Educated Christians of this period were neither unaware nor unaffected by these developments in philosophy and science. It would have been foolish of them, they knew, to try to argue down Newton's vast, mathematically ordered universe by citing a few passages from Genesis, and they had no desire to do so. Indeed, the world of natural philosophy and reason had its appeals for them, too, and so some began to argue that there were actually two ways to know God, two sacred "books," the book of scriptural revelation and the book of nature. When people of faith read the Scriptures, God's truths were revealed to them. Then, when they turned to the world of nature and looked with their own eyes and with the powers of reason, the scriptural truths were confirmed. If the Bible proclaimed that "the heavens declare the glory of God," then all one needed to do was to look through a telescope at the wondrous and harmonious stars and planets whirling in their orbits to know this to be true.[19] Newton, in fact, thought of his scientific work in just such terms. He said that when he wrote his *Principia* about the system of the universe, "I had an eye upon such principles as might work when considering men for a belief in the Deity, and nothing can rejoin me more than finding it useful for that purpose."[20]

It is a charming thought, no doubt, to imagine that the Book of Scripture and the Book of Nature sing in beautiful harmony of the glory of God, but much lies in the eye of the beholder. Believers can find God revealed in the Bible, and Enlightenment philosophers can find evidence of the deity in nature. Both may speak of God, but hidden beneath this seeming accord lies a nasty contradiction, and when we look more closely, we quickly realize they aren't talking about the same God. The God who presides as Grand Architect over the natural world, the God of Enlightenment theism, is a philosophical construct, a deity who, to use

18. See Michael J. Buckley, *At the Origins of Modern Atheism* (New Haven, Conn.: Yale University Press, 1990), p. 39.

19. See, for example, the discussion of Cotton Mather's use of "The Twofold Book of God" in Michael J. Buckley, *Denying and Disclosing God: The Ambiguous Progress of Modern Atheism* (New Haven, Conn.: Yale University Press, 2004), pp. 38-40.

20. Isaac Newton, as cited in Buckley, *At the Origins of Modern Atheism*, p. 41.

WHAT SHALL WE SAY?

theologian Walter Kasper's phrase, is an "abstract . . . unipersonal God who stands over against [humanity] as the perfect Thou."[21] The Enlightenment, with its emphasis on the power of reason and the prowess of the human mind, managed to redefine God in its own image, God as a Being among other beings, a magnified version of humanity at its best. If we are capable of moral good, then God is our morality to the nth degree. If we are powerful, then God is our kind of power to the maximum. If we are rational beings, then God is perfect rationality. If we show our genius in the design of a steam engine, then God's genius is revealed in the design of the universe, and God stands outside of this ordered creation as the Cosmic Orderer and Manager.

One problem with the God of the Enlightenment, however, is that the idea of God as the Supreme and Benevolent Architect and Manager is doomed to obsolescence. The more we know about the cosmos, the clearer it becomes that its energies and movements spring from within, not without, and the less we require a divine Supervisor. Laplace was right about the God of theism: ultimately we have no need for that hypothesis. Likewise, the more we know about the wild processes of nature — the untamed earthquakes, floods, and hurricanes — the less orderly and benign nature appears, calling into question the whole idea of a benevolent Designer beaming proudly over the best of all possible worlds. Ironically, theism is just a few inevitable dance steps away from atheism. As theologian William J. Buckley has argued, Enlightenment thinkers, choking on revealed religion, invented theism, with its God of Reason, as a remedy to preserve the possibility of belief, but the cure was worse than the disease, and the medicine ended up slaying God.[22]

By contrast, the God of the Bible is not a Being among other beings or some abstract First Cause. The biblical God cannot be fully described as "in the world" or "outside of the world." Better to say that the world is inside the love of God. The God of theism, as E. A. Burtt has reminded us, is a "cosmic conservative" interested only in maintaining the already perfectly ordered creation. "The day of novelty is all in the past: there is no

---

21. Walter Kasper, *The God of Jesus Christ* (London: SCM Press, 1984), p. 294.
22. Buckley argues this in *At the Origins of Modern Atheism* and *Denying and Disclosing God*.

further advance in time . . . no new creative activity — to this routine of temporal housekeeping is the Deity at present confined."²³ The God of Scripture, on the other hand, constantly gathers all of creation and all of human life into God's ceaseless and loving creativity. As Terry Eagleton has said,

> To say that [God] brought [the creation] into being *ex nihilo* is not a measure of how very clever he is, but to suggest that he did it out of love rather than need. The world was not the consequence of an inexorable chain of cause and effect. Like a Modernist work of art, there is no necessity about it at all, and God might well have come to regret his handiwork some aeons ago. The Creation is the original *acte gratuit*. God is an artist who did it for the sheer love or hell of it, not a scientist at work on a magnificently rational design that will impress his research grant body no end.²⁴

We can now begin to see the character of this second warning, the reason why some theologians caution us away from the theodicy highway. To allow the philosophers to frame the question is finally to flirt with idolatry and atheism. The inescapable problem, as they see it, is bound up in the very way we frame the theodicy problem, as "impossible chess match":

1. There is a God.
2. God is all-powerful.
3. God is loving and good.
4. There is innocent suffering.

But the "God" who shows up in this equation is the God of theism, the God of the Enlightenment, the mathematical First Cause of the philosophers, and not the God of Jesus Christ. Thus, the only answer possible to the theodicy problem, when it is posed this way, is a mathematical,

23. E. A. Burtt, *The Metaphysical Foundations of Modern Science*, 2d rev. ed. (London: Routledge & Kegan Paul, 1932), p. 293.

24. Terry Eagleton, "Lunging, Flailing, Mispunching," *London Review of Books* 28, no. 20 (19 October 2006): 33.

philosophical "solution" involving an abstract conception of God, a view unknown to Christian faith. Indeed, contemplating the theodicy question in this way is playing poker against the house, since this whole philosophical casting of the issue is stacked, as people like Bart Ehrman have discovered, toward the elimination of the claim "There is a God," toward atheism.

Imagine a man who confides to a friend that he is experiencing, for the first time, a crisis in his marriage. His marriage has been a happy one, a mutual sharing of love and regard. He and his wife have delighted in making life a joy for the other, but now, suddenly and inexplicably, his wife has begun occasionally to speak bitterly toward him and to act in antagonistic ways. The man confesses to his friend that he is puzzled and troubled by this new behavior and has been trying to figure out for himself why this is happening. If his friend responded by asking if he had, in fact, made any headway in discerning the reason, I suspect he would be astonished if the husband responded, "Yes, if my wife is good and loving, she must be powerless to stop this behavior, but if my wife is powerful enough to control her behavior, she must not really be good and loving, and, since she cannot be both powerful and good, I have decided that my wife doesn't exist."

The example is ridiculous, of course, because the question of the wife's existence is not even on the table. The man's wife is the one who shares his bed, who faces him each morning at breakfast, the mother of their children. Indeed, the fact that the man has a wife is what prompts the "why" question in the first place. Only if "wife" means something outside the man's reality, a hypothetical construct, could the question of her existence be germane: "I believe that there is, watching over my life, a good and powerful wife whose nature it is to arrange my life in delightful ways, but since my life is not now delightful, then no such wife exists."

Just so, in the Bible, God's existence is not a question up for grabs but the undeniable reality that gets all other questions going. In an enchanted world, God is encountered in prayer, in the rustling of the wind in the trees, in the face of the stranger, and in the garden at the cool of the day. The Bible does not ask, "I see that the wicked prosper. I wonder if there's a God?" but "O God, why do the wicked prosper?" As Paul Tillich once put it, "God cannot be reached if he is the *object* of the question and not its *basis.*"[25] Another way to say this is that, for Christians, all theological questions are forms of prayer. Enlightenment thinkers may have engaged in "reason seeking to make decisions about the existence of God," but St. Anselm described his own theological quest for God instead as "faith seeking understanding," an activity begun not in one's head but on one's knees. Philosopher John Caputo paraphrases Anselm's prayer: "Where are you, Lord? If I have wandered far away from home and gotten lost, I ask *where* my home is. I have no doubt that it is there." Caputo then contrasts this with the post-Enlightenment approach to religious questions:

> So, in modernity, the question of God is profoundly recast. Instead of beginning on our knees, we are all seated solemnly and with stern faces on the benches of the court of Reason as it is called into session. God is brought before the court, like a defendant with his hat in his hand, and required to give an account of Himself, to show His ontological papers if He expects to win the court's approval. In such a world, from Anselm's point of view, God is already dead, even if you conclude that the proof is valid, because whatever you think you have proven or disproven is not the God he experiences in prayer and liturgy but a philosophical idol. Is there or is there not a sufficient reason for this being to be?, the court wants to know. If there are reasons, are they empirical or a priori? Are they good or bad? That is what the court has assembled to decide. What does the defendant have to say for himself? What's that you say? Nothing but a few hymns, some pious prayers, and a bit of incense? Whom can he call in his defense? Shakers and Quakers and Spirit-seers all in heat? Next case![26]

Those theologians who say that the whole theodicy quest is contaminated from the outset by theistic presumptions have a point. If, as preachers, we are imaging our hearers to be detached rationalists who, arms

25. Paul Tillich, "The Two Types of Philosophy of Religion," in *Paul Tillich, Main Works: Writings in the Philosophy of Religion*, vol. 4 (Berlin: Walter de Gruyter, 1987), p. 290.

26. John D. Caputo, *On Religion* (New York: Routledge, 2001), p. 46.

crossed over their chests, are waiting on someone to solve "the impossible chess match" before they decide about the existence of God, then we are indeed on a snipe hunt. Even if we were to race from the study to the pulpit, waving a sheaf of papers and exclaiming "I have solved the theodicy problem!" the quotient of belief would probably not budge an inch. People fall in love with God, not with mathematical solutions.

Despite the warning of contamination, however, I am still persuaded that we have much to gain from exploring responses to the theodicy problem. I have two main reasons for thinking this way. First, "the impossible chess match" is, in fact, the way that many thoughtful Christians today ponder the question of suffering in the world, and, as preachers, we do not have the luxury of avoiding the question. Biblical preaching sometimes calls the culture's questions into question, but it takes the culture's questions seriously. We may well wish to change the theodicy question as it is framed, but, if so, we must walk with our hearers from where they are to this new place, and not simply declare at the outset that their quest is improper.

Second, I am not convinced that, when twenty-first-century Christians pose the theodicy question, they are suddenly reverting to the Age of Reason and the posture of Enlightenment philosophers. Like all other people, Christians need a fairly coherent view of life simply to be able to plan the day and go about the business of living. Animals have a world; human beings, like other animals, also have a world, but humans require more than an environment — we require meaning as well — and we must build a meaningful world. "Every human society," writes sociologist Peter L. Berger, "is an enterprise of world-building."[27] We have a lot of help; we do not build alone, and all of the angles do not have to be perfectly square and the joints don't have to meet perfectly — life is never as neat as that — but a person's worldview does have to be reasonably sturdy to support the confidence and sense of meaning necessary for human beings to thrive. If something breaks down in one's view of life — if, say, friends betray us or suddenly dropped objects begin to rise instead of fall — then this is a worldview crisis that must be addressed.

Berger labels a person's sense of order of the world as a "nomos," and

27. Berger, *The Sacred Canopy*, p. 3.

he connects this matter of worldview to the question of theodicy when he says,

> Every nomos . . . implies a theodicy. Every nomos confronts the individual as a meaningful reality that comprehends him and all his experiences. It bestows sense on his life, also on its discrepant and painful aspects. . . . In consequence, the pain becomes more tolerable, the terror less overwhelming, as the sheltering canopy of the nomos extends to cover even those experiences that may reduce the individual to howling animality.[28]

What Berger does here is to broaden the question of theodicy beyond the narrower issue of justifying God in the face of innocent suffering. Here "theodicy" is a need to maintain a workable sense of meaning and coherence in the face of experiences that challenge the consistency of one's worldview.

This understanding of theodicy comes closer, I think, to what ordinary Christian believers mean when they wonder about how to understand innocent suffering in light of their faith. The questions may be posed in language that sounds hypothetical — "If God is good and all-powerful, then why is there innocent suffering?" — but the need is actually more practical. "What do I say to myself, and to others, about the goodness of God when newborn babies are drowned in the floodwaters of Hurricane Katrina? I think of the world, and I think of myself, as enveloped in the love and mercy of God, but where is the merciful God when an earthquake brings down the walls of a cathedral on terrified worshipers?"

The task of theodicy, then, is not to solve a logical problem in philosophy but instead to repair a faithful but imperiled worldview. The danger we face is less that we will flirt with atheism and more that we will find ways to shore up that which should not be fortified. Berger observes:

> One of the very important social functions of theodicies is . . . their explanation of the socially prevailing inequalities of power and privilege. In this function, of course, theodicies directly legitimate the particular institutional order in question. . . . Put simply,

28. Berger, *The Sacred Canopy,* pp. 54-55.

55

theodicies provide the poor with a meaning for their poverty, but may also provide the rich with a meaning for their wealth.[29]

This caution brings us back around to our first warning: that we will explain innocent suffering in such a way that its place in the world is somehow justified. To do so is to perform the function of Job's friends rather than to follow Jesus in the way of the cross.

So, with cautions noted, we head now, eyes and ears open, into the territory of theodicy.

29. Berger, *The Sacred Canopy,* p. 59.

CHAPTER FOUR

Fellow Pilgrims

ᕊᕊ

"It is the final proof of God's omnipotence that he need not exist in order to save us."

The Reverend Andrew Mackerel in the comic novel
The Mackerel Plaza by Peter De Vries[1]

This is God's House. Be welcome to this House, whosoever you are — whether of this household or of another way, or wanderers or deserters — be welcome here. But you who are of the household, pray for us now, for us and for all sinners here or departed, that mercy draws us all one little pace nearer to Love's unveiled and dazzling face.

Sign on the door of an old church in England[2]

It has been over a half-century since the philosopher J. L. Mackie proved conclusively that a good and powerful God does not exist.

1. Peter De Vries, *The Mackerel Plaza* (Boston: Little, Brown & Co., 1958), p. 8.
2. I am grateful to David Johnson for pointing me to this quotation.

That's a bit of an exaggeration, of course. What Mackie did do was to demonstrate, through a piece of steel-trap logic highly persuasive to many, that anyone who wished to believe in a God who was both good and all-powerful, given the presence of evil in the world, was being, frankly, irrational. Mackie had, he claimed, done the math, and his dispassionately argued case was that traditional believers were not just clinging to an outdated piety, as a secular critic might charge, or courageously stepping out in faith beyond all evidence, as the believers themselves might contend, but being just flat illogical. Mackie's essay on this theme, "Evil and Omnipotence,"[3] now a classic of philosophical discourse, appeared to produce a knockdown argument that what we have called "the impossible chess match" is, in fact, truly impossible and nothing but a dead end. Given Mackie's reasoning, not only is the theodicy problem hopelessly unworkable, but also, by implication, the whole business of belief in God is in serious logical trouble, too.

Mackie was a brilliant and learned man, and an outspoken atheist. Long before *The God Delusion,* Richard Dawkins's fists-up attack on "the interventionist, miracle-wreaking, thought-reading, sin-punishing, prayer-answering God of the Bible,"[4] Mackie, a far more gentle spirit, had done Dawkins's job for him by laying out a seemingly airtight case that people who say that God is loving, just, and powerful are spouting nonsense because the claims involve inescapable contradictions, a genuine God delusion. Of course, people could go on believing in God if they wished; Mackie's argument did nothing to damage that possibility. But the cost was high. Logically, one could believe in God only by being willing to give up on the notion that God is both morally good and all-powerful. But for many traditional Christians, God's moral goodness and omnipotence are part of the package along with God's existence. One claim goes, and the rest go with it.

Particularly impressive about Mackie's essay was the way in which he had ostensibly delivered a fatal blow to one of the favorite arguments that people employ to wriggle free of the theodicy problem — namely,

3. J. L. Mackie, "Evil and Omnipotence," in *The Problem of Evil,* ed. Marilyn McCord Adams and Robert Merrihew Adams (New York: Oxford University Press, 1990), pp. 25-37.

4. Richard Dawkins, *The God Delusion* (New York: Mariner Books, 2006), p. 41.

the so-called free-will defense. Essentially, this is the claim that, yes, there is evil in the world, but it is not God's doing or fault. Evil is due entirely to the exercise of human free will (and, in some versions, also the free will of angels and other creatures). God cannot be blamed for evil, directly or even indirectly, because if humanity had not been given freedom of will, human beings would simply be automatons.

In regard to this argument, Mackie went right for the jugular. He refused to let God off the hook, claiming that the so-called free-will defense was no defense at all. To call God omnipotent, Mackie reasoned, meant what it said, that God possessed infinite possibilities, could in fact do anything God chose to do. Therefore, an all-powerful God could logically have created a world in which human beings could be completely free in their choices but would freely choose the good on each and every occasion. "Clearly, his failure to avail himself of this possibility," Mackie said, "is inconsistent with his being both omnipotent and wholly good."[5]

Case closed? Not quite. The faithful, of course, went on lighting candles, saying prayers, and singing the doxology to a good and sovereign God, unaware that Mackie and others convinced by his essay were confident that what they were doing was futile and irrational. But then, a Christian philosopher by the name of Alvin Plantinga took up Mackie's challenge by mounting a spirited justification of the free-will defense. Plantinga's argument is, like Mackie's, a brilliant, highly logical piece of reasoning, laid down plank by plank, and, as such, is not easily summarized. At the heart of the case, however, is Plantinga's claim that Mackie was operating with a flawed definition of "omnipotence" — namely, that omnipotence means that God can do anything God pleases, no holds barred. Plantinga counters that even an omnipotent God cannot generate states of affairs that violate the rules of logic, cannot create, for example, square circles or married bachelors.[6] In fact, Plantinga argued, believers have never meant by "omnipotence" that God could make a rock so big that God couldn't lift it. Although Plantinga does not here cite Aquinas, the same argument had been advanced in the thirteenth century in Thomas's *Summa Theologica*:

5. Mackie, "Evil and Omnipotence," p. 33.
6. Alvin Plantinga, *God, Freedom, and Evil* (New York: Harper & Row, 1974), p. 17.

All confess that God is omnipotent; but it seems difficult to explain in what His omnipotence precisely consists: for there may be doubt as to the precise meaning of the word "all" when we say that God can do all things. If, however, we consider the matter aright, since power is said in reference to possible things, this phrase, "God can do all things," is rightly understood to mean that God can do all things that are possible; and for this reason He is said to be omnipotent.[7]

Plantinga agrees: "What the theist typically means when he says that God is omnipotent is not that there are *no* limits to God's power, but at most that there are no nonlogical limits."[8]

Plantinga's clarification of the meaning of omnipotence allowed him to pick the lock on Mackie's argument. Mackie claimed that God, since God has infinite possibilities, could, if he desired, have created a world populated by free creatures who never did anything morally evil, who would always have chosen the good. Plantinga countered that such creatures would be like orphans with parents, illogical and outside the bounds of even an omnipotent God to create. "Free" creatures who are programmed by God always to choose the good implies divine causality in those choices, which logically contradicts the concept of freedom:

> Now God can create free creatures, but He can't *cause* or *determine* them to do only what is right. For if He does so, then they aren't significantly free after all; they do not do what is right *freely.* To create creatures capable of *moral good,* therefore, He must create creatures capable of moral evil, and he can't give these creatures the freedom to perform evil and at the same time prevent them from doing so. As it turned out, sadly enough, some of the free creatures God created went wrong in the exercise of their freedom; this is the source of moral evil.[9]

---

7. Thomas Aquinas, *The Summa Theologica of St. Thomas Aquinas,* 2d rev. ed., 1.25.3, online edition copyright © 2008 by Kevin Knight, http://www.newadvent.org/summa/1025.htm#article3.

8. Plantinga, *God, Freedom, and Evil,* p. 18.

9. Plantinga, *God, Freedom, and Evil,* p. 30.

Not everyone agrees with Plantinga's theology, naturally, but his logical refutation of Mackie is hard to get around. Most philosophers today are, in fact, persuaded that Plantinga found the weak point in Mackie's case, and philosopher Stephen Davis has noted that it is "largely due to the work of Plantinga that one rarely hears any longer the problem of evil presented as if it were a purely logical problem, as if theists are contradicting themselves."[10] The case for God in a world of evil still needs to be made, of course, but because of Plantinga's work, at least the case cannot be laughed out of court as logically incoherent.

But clear logic sometimes makes for cold comfort. To say that it is not irrational to claim both (a) that God is omnipotent, loving, and just, and (b) that innocent suffering and evil exist in the world is a far cry from saying something true and reassuring to a thinking Christian puzzled over how so much suffering could happen in a world where a loving God has the power to act, not to mention saying something true and reassuring to that Sri Lankan father who lost four of his children in the tsunami. Thinkers like Plantinga have opened the door. They have shown that exploring the theodicy question is not a *prima facie* exercise in irrationality. But the search is not just for logic, but for credible ways to understand this challenge to faith. Our task now is to explore several representative approaches that faithful people have tried to find these credible ways, to address theodicy in a pastoral as well as a logical way. We will engage in open — but also critical — conversations with fellow pilgrims who seek to understand the love and presence of God in a suffering world. We will begin not with the oldest response to the problem, but instead with a fairly recent response to theodicy, an approach that millions of people have found convincing and helpful: Rabbi Harold Kushner's *When Bad Things Happen to Good People.*

10. Stephen T. Davis, "Free Will and Evil," in *Encountering Evil: Live Options in Theodicy,* new ed., ed. Stephen T. Davis (Louisville: Westminster John Knox Press, 2001), p. 74.

When Bad Things Happen to Good People

Rabbi Harold Kushner's 1981 best seller, *When Bad Things Happen to Good People*,[11] is a book of popular theology that needs to be taken seriously if for no other reason than it has been received by many readers with such gratitude and acclaim. Just as Leslie Weatherhead's *The Will of God* did for the World War II generation, Kushner's book has provided a way through the problem of evil that is persuasive and comforting for so many in our time. The very first paragraph of the book both gives us a clue to its popularity and serves as wise counsel for those who preach on this theme:

> This is not an abstract book about God and theology. It does not try to use big words or clever ways of rephrasing questions in an effort to convince us that our problems are not really problems, but that we only think they are. This is a very personal book, written by someone who believes in God and in the goodness of the world, someone who has spent most of his life trying to help other people believe, and was compelled by a personal tragedy to rethink everything he had been taught about God and God's ways.[12]

What prompted Kushner's book was indeed a personal tragedy: the death of his son Aaron from progeria, a rare and universally fatal genetic disease which has, among other symptoms, the appearance of rapid aging. When Aaron was three years old, Kushner and his wife were told by their physician that their son would grow to be only about three feet tall, would have no hair on his head or body, would look like an old person even in his early childhood, and would die in his early teens. The physician was correct; Aaron experienced all of these manifestations and died at age fourteen.

Among Kushner's several reactions to this terrible diagnosis was a sense of moral outrage at God for the unfairness of it all. Kushner and his wife were ethical people, people with more religious commitment than many others. And even if Kushner had overlooked some moral offense

---

11. Harold Kushner, *When Bad Things Happen to Good People* (New York: Avon, 1981).

12. Kushner, *When Bad Things Happen to Good People*, p. 1.

that made him deserving of God's punishment, the same could not be said for Aaron. "He was an innocent child, a happy outgoing three-year-old. Why should he have to suffer physical and psychological pain every day of his life? Why should he have to be stared at, pointed at, wherever he went? Why should he be condemned to grow into adolescence, see other boys and girls beginning to date, and realize that he would never know marriage or fatherhood?"[13] This was not the way God's world was supposed to work.

Kushner set out to find an answer to his question: Why? Standing behind his quest is the familiar framing of the problem as "the impossible chess match." Kushner had always believed that God is just and fair and that God is all-powerful, but he could no longer square these beliefs with the undeserved suffering of his own son. Divine love and power cannot be reconciled with innocent suffering. Something had to give.[14]

Kushner became acquainted over time with many of the stock-in-trade answers and explanations for innocent suffering, the kind of pious sayings that people have relied on for comfort through the centuries — God gives people what they deserve, or God uses suffering to build our knowledge and character, or suffering fits in ways we do not yet see into God's greater design. Again, a strength of Kushner's book is the way in which he honestly and systematically exposes each of them as empty comfort. He is like the biblical Job railing at his friends, "I used to say the same things as you. I, too, have spoken those old bromides, but my own suffering now renders these answers false."

For example, in rejecting the notion that suffering is sent to us somehow to strengthen us, to build character, he tells the story of Harriet Schiff, whose young son died in surgery to correct a congenital heart problem. Her pastor took her aside and said, "I know this is a painful time for you. But I know you'll get through it all right, because God never sends us more of a burden than we can bear." Which Harriet heard to mean that, if only she had been a weaker person, her son Robbie would still be alive.[15]

---

13. Kushner, *When Bad Things Happen to Good People*, pp. 2-3.
14. See Kushner, *When Bad Things Happen to Good People*, p. 37.
15. Kushner, *When Bad Things Happen to Good People*, p. 16.

Kushner also pushes away eschatological explanations, reassurances that suffering is a great mystery to us now, but one day the reasons for it will be made clear. We'll understand it better by and by. He describes the image of a great tapestry that Thornton Wilder develops in the novel *The Eighth Day*. Human life, suggests Wilder, is like this tapestry. Seen from the "good" side, it displays a pattern of great beauty and intricacy, God's grand design, but we experience life from the other side, the "under" side of the tapestry, a seeming confusion of broken threads and loose ends. We cannot yet see what one day we will see — how the very fragments and brokenness of life are, in fact, contributing to the great design. One life is lived in relative health and peacefulness, while another life is abruptly cut short, not because one is more deserving than the other, but because the great pattern demands it. This is, Kushner sniffs, at best "a hypothetical solution to a real problem." The sufferings of humanity are real. "We have seen them," says Kushner. "But nobody has seen Wilder's tapestry."[16]

Having searched the standard array of responses to the theodicy problem, Kushner dismisses them all. What they have in common, Kushner observes, is that they begin with the assumption that God is somehow the cause of human suffering. Maybe God has reasons for allowing us to suffer — to build character, perhaps, or to teach us a lesson — or maybe God is simply uncaring, dishing out pain indifferent to our plight. But all of the typical explanations, Kushner discovered, see the hand of God behind human suffering.

Not satisfied by any of the customary answers, Kushner ventured out on his own to find a different response to the question of why God allowed his son to suffer so terribly. He turned for help, as many others have, to the book of Job, which he calls "the most profound and complete consideration of human suffering in the Bible."[17] After reviewing the story of Job and exploring the interactions between Job and God, Kushner made, he claimed, a startling discovery. In one of the "speeches out of the whirlwind" that God delivers to Job near the end of the book, Kushner found what he believes is the author of Job's solution to the im-

---

16. Kushner, *When Bad Things Happen to Good People*, p. 18.
17. Kushner, *When Bad Things Happen to Good People*, p. 30.

possible chess match, to the agonizing question of how a good God could allow innocent people to suffer horribly. The solution Kushner found was that God is loving and just, but God is simply not powerful enough to banish all evil and suffering. Why doesn't God stop all suffering? Because God can't. According to Kushner's reading of the book of Job, God is simply not strong enough to bring suffering to an end.

The speech that Kushner finds so insightful is a portion of Job 40, which Kushner identifies, somewhat eccentrically, as perhaps "the most important lines in the whole book."[18] In this passage, God says to Job,

> Have you an arm like God?
> Can you thunder with a voice like His?
> *You* tread down the wicked where they stand.
> Bury them in the dust together . . .
> Then will I acknowledge that your own right hand can
>   give you victory.[19]

Now, the divine speeches in the book of Job have, in Carol Newsom's nice phrase, a "teasing resistance" to being understood.[20] It is hard to know whether to imagine them being thundered from on high or whispered with quiet and wise irony, but, despite the many difficulties in interpreting these passages, most students of the book of Job see things differently than Kushner does. Despite the uncertainties involved, the majority of biblical scholars think that the basic thrust of the speech in Job 40 is clear enough. God is contrasting human weakness with divine power, saying something like, "Do you think you are my equal, Job, that you can defeat evil with your own puny human strength, that you can save yourself? If so, just try it." Kushner, however, hears something different in this text. He understands God to be saying, "Job, I am doing the best I can, but I am not in control of all this. Managing evil is not an easy task, even for me, and so, Job, 'if you think it's so easy to keep the world

---

18. Kushner, *When Bad Things Happen to Good People,* p. 43.

19. This version of the passage is comprised of selected phrases from Job 40:9-14, apparently paraphrased.

20. Carol A. Newsom, *The Book of Job: A Contest of Moral Imaginations* (New York: Oxford University Press, 2003), p. 235.

straight and true, to keep unfair things from happening to people, *you* try it.'"[21]

One gets the impression that this is not really an exegetical insight for Kushner.[22] This is an idea to which he has been driven, and he hammers this text from Job to fit what he has already decided must be true. In short, in the impossible chess match, Kushner's options are limited. He knows firsthand that there is innocent suffering, and he will not give up his belief in a loving and just God. And so the only chess piece he has to sacrifice is a belief in the omnipotence of God. Kushner says,

> I no longer hold God responsible for illnesses, accidents, and natural disasters, because I realize that I gain little and I lose so much when I blame God for those things. I can worship a God who hates suffering but cannot eliminate it, more easily than I can worship a God who chooses to make children suffer and die, for whatever exalted reason.[23]

So if God is not responsible for evil, then where, in Kushner's view, does it come from? Some of it arises out of sheer bad luck, he suggests, some from the cruel acts of immoral people, but most of it comes from the randomness of nature and from fate. "Fate, not God, sends us the problem."[24]

Kushner's popular response to the theodicy problem has been pasto-

---

21. Kushner, *When Bad Things Happen to Good People*, p. 43.

22. Abraham Cohen, analyzing *When Bad Things Happen to Good People* in *Modern Judaism*, agrees. He goes further to suggest that Kushner actually has little real interest in biblical theology and that the insight Kushner claimed to have gleaned from the book of Job was not vital in Kushner's argument. "Our reason for saying that Job is not crucial to Kushner's case is this: Kushner stands independent of biblical theology. This is a fact evident from all of Kushner's writings. In the previous chapter [of *When Bad Things Happen to Good People*], e.g., Kushner was quick to demur from several biblical texts which declared the operation of strict justice in the world. . . . And, so, we suggest that had Job presented a position antithetical to that of Kushner, he could have comfortably dismissed it, and proceeded to offer his own position." See Abraham Cohen, "Theology and Theodicy: Reading Harold Kushner," *Modern Judaism* 16, no. 3 (October 1996): 231-32.

23. Kushner, *When Bad Things Happen to Good People*, p. 134.

24. Kushner, *When Bad Things Happen to Good People*, p. 129.

rally helpful to many people and a great relief especially to those who have themselves experienced a tragedy. Kushner reassures them that God did not cause this suffering, that God is not punishing them for some misdeed, and that God would have stopped the pain and grief if it were in God's power to do so. But how does Kushner's approach to the theodicy problem hold up theologically? Theologian Douglas John Hall is critical of Kushner on at least two basic points. Hall's first criticism, although he would probably resist this description of it, is essentially a Protestant objection to Kushner's use of the terms "good" and "bad." To talk about "bad" things happening to "good" people is, Hall charges, morally truncated. "Bad" things don't always turn out to be bad, and "good" people are, in the Pauline sense, not all that good. This causes Kushner's moral categories of good and bad to be insufficiently nuanced and — here is the key thing for Hall — allows Kushner's book to be read by "average 'good' middle-class North Americans *without ever causing them to question their fundamental assumptions about themselves and their society.*" If we are offended that suffering happens to good people like us, Hall charges, we are preoccupied by our own sense of righteousness and never are able, like Isaiah, to see ourselves as people "of unclean lips living in the midst of a people of unclean lips."[25]

Actually, I'm going with Kushner, and against Hall, on this one. I know the Pauline dictum — "all have sinned and fall short of the glory of God" — but that seems beside the point here. Yes, none of us can claim, finally, to be "good people," and Kushner's definitions of "good" and "bad" are rough-cut, but Kushner is not trying to make the argument that his personal righteousness merited special protection from God. In the context of Kushner's book, being "good" means mainly living the kind of life that trusts that the world is built on the goodness and justice of God. Kushner's moral issue is that a child dying of a dreadful disease before he's had a chance to sing his song, and his parents trying to serve God and collapsing in grief, bewilderment, and agony, is all out of proportion to whatever moral failings any of them may have. In short, however one defines "good people" or "bad people," none of it helps explain why

25. Douglas John Hall, *God and Human Suffering: An Exercise in the Theology of the Cross* (Minneapolis: Augsburg Press, 1986), p. 154.

Kushner's son was inflicted with his horrible disease. Surely the goodness of God must mean that in some measure the universe has moral stability, and surely the love of God can find a way to teach ethics, discipline creatures, and provoke repentance without killing helpless children to make an ethical point. I hear Kushner saying, in his own rabbinical way, essentially what Jesus said: If we, "who are evil, know how to give good gifts" to our children, how much more will God do so (Luke 11:13).

What is admirable about Kushner is his refusal to make God the author of evil and suffering. Kushner has faith in a loving and just God, and he is not going to cross his fingers and find some way to embrace his own son's illness and death as somehow an expression of that divine love and justice. This puts him in a logical bind, and the only way he can see out of it is to yield on God's omnipotence. Where Kushner gets into trouble, I think, is in the collateral damage done by this doctrine of God. Monstrous evil must come from somewhere, he thinks, and for Kushner it finally comes from Fate — that's Fate with a capital "F." Fate, for Kushner, is more than just the random turning of a neutral and indifferent nature; it is an active force. The notion that God sends trouble into human life is wrong, he says. "Fate, not God, sends the problem."[26] It was Fate that took the life of his son. Fate was there at the beginning of creation; fate is the power of random chaos, and God cannot tame it.

Unwittingly, then, Kushner has set up a second cosmic force, a rival to God, and, as Hall points out as his second criticism, fallen into a good-God, bad-God cosmic dualism.[27] This is essentially the posture of Gnosticism. The ancient Gnostics, challenged in their own way by an early form of the theodicy problem, were alarmed that the material world was filled with unjustified suffering. They finally concluded that God could not be the author of this conflicted creation. So, it must have come from a lesser deity, the Demiurge. Kushner's "Fate" comes perilously close to a renaming of the Demiurge. Faced with a blind Fate that promiscuously slings suffering at humanity and a weak God who "inspires people to help other people who have been hurt" but can do little else, Kushner is thrown back on human potential. The bad things that

26. Kushner, *When Bad Things Happen to Good People*, p. 129.
27. Hall, *God and Human Suffering*, p. 155.

happen to us don't have any meaning, "but *we* can give them a meaning. We can redeem these tragedies from senselessness by imposing meaning on them."[28] According to Kushner, then, when it comes to evil and suffering, redemption is something *we* do, not God. God may help us, but the task is essentially ours. This is a brave view, perhaps, but it also involves an impoverished understanding of God, and that, as Hall puts it, "is theologically and humanly unsatisfying."[29]

When one strips away all of the biblical language and the pastoral talk from Kushner's book, what remains is fairly stark. We live in a world where random Fate causes suffering and pain to occur promiscuously, and other than sending out Hallmark-style inspirations for people to have courage and work together, God can do little about it. What is left for good people in the midst of suffering is to gird up their loins and to face life bravely, with a willingness to accept the hand that reality deals them and to do what they can to make the world better. Worthy of Sartre, perhaps, but faith promises more.

There is a certain affinity between where Kushner comes out on theodicy and the place where Bart Ehrman finally arrives when he embraces what he understands to be the view of the writer of Ecclesiastes: Life is a mystery, and much of it doesn't make sense; don't expect justice, since good people sometimes lose and bad people sometimes win; bad things happen at random, but good things do, too; so seize this transitory life and enjoy as much of it as you can.[30] The moral compass swings wildly in such a worldview, and there is no guarantee where it will ultimately point. Kushner, at least, turns outward, toward others and toward faith in God. Ehrman turns inward:

> I think we should work hard to make the world — the one we live in — the most pleasing place it can be *for ourselves*. We should love and be loved. We should cultivate our friendships, enjoy our intimate relationships, cherish our family lives. We should make money and spend money. The more the better. We should enjoy

28. Kushner, *When Bad Things Happen to Good People*, p. 136, emphasis added.
29. Hall, *God and Human Suffering*, p. 157.
30. Bart D. Ehrman, *God's Problem: How the Bible Fails to Answer Our Most Important Question — Why We Suffer* (New York: HarperOne, 2008), p. 276.

good food and drink. We should eat out and enjoy unhealthy desserts, and we should cook steaks on the grill and drink Bordeaux. We should walk around the block, work in the garden, watch basketball and drink beer. We should travel and read books and go to museums and look at art and listen to music. We should drive nice cars and have nice homes. We should make love, have babies, and raise families. We should do what we can to love life — it's a gift and will not be with us for long.[31]

The poverty of such advice becomes clear when we imagine it being spoken to any congregation with the usual quotient of deep wounds and silent sufferings. Even more, its effete elitism hardens into cruelty in the context of the Haitian earthquake or the Indian Ocean tsunami. What kind of moral numbskull would clasp a hand across the shoulder of a man who had lost his family to the surging waters and say, "I think you should cook a steak on the grill, have a glass of Bordeaux, and take in the ACC basketball tournament. Love life — it's a gift and will not be with us for long."

Process Thought

Kushner makes the impossible chess match move forward by yielding on the omnipotence of God. American process theologians work the same territory, but not by making God weaker, per se, but instead by radically changing the definition of power. Process theologian John Cobb charges that much theology envisions God's power like that of a potter with clay. The potter decides how to shape the clay, and the potter molds the clay by force as the potter will. Of course, the picture of God as a potter raises the theodicy problems sharply. When something goes wrong, when tragedy strikes, when the "pot" is misshapen, why doesn't God reach in and reshape the clay?

But to imagine that God's power is like this, says Cobb, is actually to reduce God's power. Frightened parents, prison guards, and tyrants may exercise this potter-and-clay kind of power, the power to force and com-

---

31. Ehrman, *God's Problem*, p. 277 (emphasis in the original).

pel, but it is finally a sign of their weakness.[32] God's power is not the power of a potter, says Cobb, but of a persuader. God's power is more like that of a wise and effective parent than a potter. God is in the mix of things, the middle of whatever there is, exercising persuasive power to maximize the good.[33]

But how does the persuader God fit in with the claim that God is "the maker of heaven and earth"? It is crucial to the view of process theology that God did not create the world *ex nihilo,* out of nothing. That's the potter-and-clay view of God, a picture of God as absolute controller.[34] No, the world was already there before God began God's creative work, before God started exercising persuasive power. Process theologians prefer a particular rendition of Genesis 1:1 — not the more familiar translation "In the beginning, when God created the heavens and the earth," but instead "When *God* began to create the heavens and the earth, the world was without form and void."[35] This translation implies that there was already something out there before God began creative activity, and it underscores a key point in process theology: none of life's circumstances is a blank slate, not even what we call "the creation," and God does not possess infinite creative possibilities. God's power is contingent upon the freedom and possibilities inherent in each circumstance. In short, God is not like an architect who gets to sketch out the perfect house on a sheet of blank paper; God is more like a remodeler, who takes an old house and makes it more livable.

Building upon concepts drawn from the philosophy of Alfred North Whitehead, process theologians see God not as "being" but as "process," ceaseless creative energy embedded in larger evolving systems. God works in and with what is available, not coercing but luring the world toward greater and greater good. Cobb imagines what we call evolution as a response to the call of this persuasive God. God called out to the

32. John B. Cobb Jr., *God and the World* (Philadelphia: Westminster Press, 1969), p. 89.

33. Cobb, *God and the World,* pp. 90-91.

34. John B. Cobb Jr. and David Ray Griffin, *Process Theology: An Introductory Exposition* (Philadelphia: Westminster Press, 1976), p. 65.

35. David Ray Griffin, "Creation Out of Nothing, Creation Out of Chaos and the Problem of Evil," in *Encountering Evil,* new ed., ed. Davis, p. 108.

primordial mud, summoning it to become animal life, and then to the animals:

> God called, "Leave the mud, stand up, give birth to your betters!"
>   The animals resist: "We don't want to! We can't!"
>   But God insists: "You can't but I can. Stand up!"
>   And lo, after thousands of eons, [humanity] emerged, trembling on . . . still unsolid legs.[36]

Cobb claims that a process view of God's loving and persuasive power basically solves, or at least minimizes, the problem of natural evil. Sure, the available world out there has earthquakes and tsunamis, but these are morally neutral events; they are just natural processes and would not be seen as evil if there were no life for them to destroy. If a fifty-foot wave rises up in the North Atlantic, no one would deem this to be an "evil" thing. But if a fishing boat is rolled under the sea by this wave and seven crew members are drowned, then we speak of tragedy and evil. The wave isn't evil; evil occurs because human life got in harm's way. But it was God who persuaded life to come forth, it was God who beckoned life to become ever more complex and eventually human, it was God who was implicated in the processes that led to a boat full of fishermen being at that spot in the ocean. Perhaps God was wrong to persuade the world to teem with life, especially the higher forms of life. God lured human life to come forth into a world that God does not have the power to control, and one result has been that humans have been exposed to terrible pain and suffering. Is God morally indictable for this? Did God, in effect, persuade us to play with fire in a room full of gas fumes?

Process theologian David Ray Griffin raises this question in his book *God, Power, and Evil: A Process Theodicy.* Should God have let the primordial unruliness be, Griffin asks, and avoided bringing order out of the chaos? Or maybe God should have stopped short of urging complex life forms forward, so that at least the higher forms of evil would not have been possible.[37] To be sure, Griffin admits, God did take deep risks with

36. Cobb, *God and the World*, p. 53.

37. David Ray Griffin, *God, Power, and Evil: A Process Theodicy* (Philadelphia: Westminster Press, 1976), p. 308.

the creation, and because of this God is "clearly responsible" for all of the moral evil in the world.[38] But anyone who wishes to shake a fist in God's face for this, Griffin argues, must at least take two important considerations into account.

First, there is the question of what constitutes evil. Critics of God's creative risking, says Griffin, assume that discord is the only form of evil, overlooking the fact that "unnecessary triviality is also genuinely evil."[39] To be sure, if God had left things well enough alone and not persuaded more complex forms of life to emerge, then intense discord would have been avoided, but the enjoyment of intense harmonies would also have been missed. No fishermen would drown in such a world, no musicians would die in plane crashes, no astronauts would perish in exploding space shuttles, but would not a world devoid of experiences such as work, music, and exploration be, Griffin argues, a lesser world, indeed filled with the evil of lifelessness and triviality? Here, Griffin advances an argument slightly reminiscent of the old Flip Wilson comedy routine in which Wilson, playing a hip version of Christopher Columbus, tells Queen Isabella of Spain that if she doesn't let him sail across the ocean to discover America, then "there ain't gonna be no Ray Charles." Griffin asks whether God should have avoided creating higher forms of life. True, there would have been no Hitler or Stalin, but there would also have been no Jesus, Mozart, Gandhi, Florence Nightingale, or Louis Armstrong, either.[40]

Second, Griffin reminds us that in process thought, God is not the God of classical theism, an impassive deity who stands outside of the experience of suffering, but a God who shares the full consequences of all risks taken with creation. The fact that God is in the muck and mire of experience with humanity, exposed to the full range of suffering, claims Griffin, eliminates any reason for anger toward God, because it

> removes the basis for that sense of moral outrage which would be directed toward an impassive spectator deity who took great risks with creation. . . . The one being who is in position to know

38. Griffin, *God, Power, and Evil*, p. 300.
39. Griffin, *God, Power, and Evil*, p. 308.
40. Griffin, *God, Power, and Evil*, p. 309.

experientially the bitter as well as the sweet fruits of the risk of creation is the same being who has encouraged and who continues to encourage this process of creative risk-taking.[41]

Process theology's God is not omnipotent. God does not have the power to mold the perfect good but only to persuade the world toward the best available option. But a world full of life, even at risk, is better than a safe but lifeless world. It may even be, given the circumstances of the primordial chaos, that God called forth life at the one possible moment that it could have developed. If God had waited to create life, this argument goes, then this one window of opportunity would have closed.[42]

What do we make of the process response to theodicy? There is something right, to be sure, in the attempt to re-imagine the idea of divine power. One could dip down here and there in the Bible and come up with a number of images of God's power contrary to process thought, where the biblical God exerts power that is more than just persuasive — for example, creating the sun and the moon, dividing the Red Sea, and changing the fortune of armies at war. Indeed, the image of God as a potter who can do whatever God wills with the clay, the image of power that John Cobb thought worthy only of a prison guard, is, in fact, a biblical image for God's power. But if Jesus is the clearest manifestation of God's power, then the truest biblical portrayal of divine power is radically different from the sheer power to mold, manipulate, or coerce.

Because of this redefinition of power, process theology also technically solves the impossible chess match. Like Kushner, process theologians' answer to the question of why God didn't prevent the Lisbon earthquake or the Indian Ocean tsunami is that it was not in God's power to do so. Like Leibniz, process thinkers believe that God is bringing into being the best of all possible worlds, but for process thought this is a work in progress, and "the best of all possible worlds" is not a state but a constantly evolving process.

But we must press the same question on process theology that we

41. Griffin, *God, Power, and Evil*, p. 310.
42. Cobb, *God and the World*, p. 93.

raised for Kushner: At what price has the theodicy problem been re-solved? Process thought has much to offer in terms of understanding creativity, aesthetics, and the connections between faith and natural sci-ence, but it finally stumbles badly, I am convinced, over theodicy. First, process theologians, like Kushner, end up mangling the doctrine of God. There is a ring of truth when the critics complain that process theolo-gians want to draw an empathetic picture of God, but they end up pro-ducing merely a pathetic one, a God one might find endearing, but not worthy of worship. Here is God in the midst of chaos, whispering, plead-ing, trying to persuade a balky world to be better, to be less trivial and more aesthetically pleasing, but the results are less than impressive. As John Roth has complained,

> At Auschwitz, the best that God could do was to permit ten thou-sand Jews a day to go up in smoke. That process had been going on for years, but remember that God was doing all that God could do to persuade a different outcome into existence. . . . A God of such weakness, no matter how much God tries to persuade, is rather pathetic. [This] God is too small . . . inspires little awe, little sense of holiness. [This] God neither deserves nor will attract much attention.[43]

Theologian Robert Neville, who in his own work refashioned some of the categories of process thought, is particularly critical of a strict Whiteheadian view of God, which he says makes God out to be some-thing like a helicopter parent, a "smother-mother," always hovering around, pleading and cajoling, "Now I can't makes these decisions for you. You have to choose for yourself, but you know what's best. I've done all I can do to make you happy, and now it's up to you to choose the best way. . . ." The God of the Bible, said Neville, is awesome and free to be ter-rible; Whitehead's God is just "nice."[44]

Second, the process God who takes risks with creation but who also

---

43. John K. Roth, "Critique," in *Encountering Evil*, p. 128.

44. Robert Neville, as cited in Gary Dorrien, *The Making of American Liberal Theol-ogy: Crisis, Irony, and Postmodernity, 1950-2005* (Louisville: Westminster John Knox Press, 2006), p. 382.

shares those risks with us, the God who is in the process with us and who "suffers with our sufferings," does not, despite Griffin's reassurances, really do much to reduce our moral outrage or provide much consolation. A God who tells the people of Lisbon, "Oops . . . well, the risk went badly there, but I want you to know that I share the risk and feel the pain" is, as one wag put it, like an intoxicated driver who slurs to his unsuspecting passengers, "This is risky, I know, but hey, I'm sharing the ride." As Karl Rahner once said in a dialogue with Jürgen Moltmann, "To put it crudely, it does not help me to escape from my mess and mix-up and despair if God is in the same predicament."[45] A God who is defined completely as one embedded in developing processes, is, as William Placher has charged, a God of "domesticated transcendence" and "not the God of Christian faith."[46] To this conception of God, Rahner put the question well: "What use would that be to me as consolation in the true sense of the word?"

Free Will

If Kushner and the process theologians want to address the theodicy question by reducing or redefining the idea of God as all-powerful, there are other Christians who in one way or another want to challenge the notion that human suffering is innocent. The oldest and most persuasive of these is, of course, Augustine, who finds the origins of evil in the free will and rebellion of God's creatures.

According to Augustine, the world that God created for us and other creatures was a perfect paradise. It wasn't too hot, and it wasn't too cold. Human beings lived without any needs, and they lived eternally. They had food and drink, and the tree of life to keep them from getting old. No one got sick; no one ever had an accident. Humans were free, free to choose, free to do good or not, but there was no need for the Ten Com-

45. Karl Rahner, "The Question of Compassion and God's Impassibility," in Jürgen Moltmann, *History and the Triune God,* trans. J. Bowden (New York: Crossroad, 1992), p. 122.
46. William C. Placher, *The Domestication of Transcendence: How Modern Thinking about God Went Wrong* (Louisville: Westminster John Knox Press, 1996), esp. pp. 7-10.

mandments; people were intuitively at one with each other and with God. There was no sadness, and also no foolish frivolity. There was work to do, but it never made them weary. There was sex, but no lust; marriage, but no battle of wills. True joy flowed from the presence of God, and God was praised and adored out of a pure heart, a good conscience, and deep faith. Paradise.[47]

But then, for reasons mysterious and bound up in the inscrutable nature of freedom, God's creatures turned away from the good, willfully turned away from God, turned in desire toward that which was not the highest good. This was not merely a human rebellion, but angels, too, turned from God, and the whole creation fell away from the goodness given by God. God had created the creatures *ex nihilo* and created them good, and now the creatures returned the favor and created evil *ex nihilo*. Technically speaking, evil has no reality; it is nothing; it is a lack, a deprivation, of the good, but like a strong vacuum, it has great power in its very nothingness. As for suffering — from death camps to earthquakes — it is all the consequence of a creation thrown into chaos by the misuse of free will. Now God's project is the salvation of a world gone awry. The impossible chess match can move forward because in a precise sense, there is no suffering that is innocent.

This so-called free-will defense is the one response to evil that seems to have most settled into the vocabulary of American Christians. It fits with popular interpretations of the Adam and Eve story and seems to make a certain kind of sense. Bart Ehrman said that when he was writing

---

47. Augustine, *The City of God,* XIV, 26. "In paradise, then, man . . . lived in the enjoyment of God, and was good by God's goodness; he lived without any want, and had it in his power to live eternally. He had food that he might not hunger, drink that he might not thirst, the tree of life that old age might not waste him. There was in his body no corruption, nor seed of corruption, which could produce in him any unpleasant sensation. He feared no inward disease, no outward accident. Soundest health blessed his body, absolute tranquility his soul. As in Paradise there was no excessive heat or cold, so its inhabitants were exempt from vicissitudes of fear and desire. No sadness of any kind was there, nor any foolish joy; true gladness ceaselessly flowed from the presence of God, who was loved 'out of pure heart, and a good conscience, and faith unfeigned.' The honest love of a husband and wife made a sure harmony between them. Body and spirit worked harmoniously together, and the commandment was kept without labor. No languor made their leisure wearisome; no sleepiness interrupted their desire to labor."

his book on suffering and would tell people, at cocktail parties and elsewhere, that he was working on why God allows so much suffering, some
people would turn away, not even wanting to talk about it. But he noted
that many others would quickly try to explain it, or would send him an
e-mail later, most of the time with the idea of free will. "If we didn't have
free will," they'd say, "we'd be like robots. And with free will comes risk."[48]

The virtue of the free-will explanation is that it succumbs neither to
determinism nor to dualism. It recognizes that human beings inhabit a
universe of moral freedom and choice and that these choices matter
greatly. Life is not predetermined by some controlling deity with the per-
sonality of a railroad timekeeper, but unfolds with a certain unpredict-
ability. Moreover, there is no Kushneresque good-God, bad-Fate battle
raging here. The power of God remains in full force, and no independent
ontological status is granted to evil. Evil is not something in and of itself,
which then has to be somehow billed to God's account, since God created all that exists; it is the lack of something, a *privatio boni,* a deprivation of the good that God intends. Moreover, Augustine's broad view is
salvific and eschatological. What that means is that God is at work in
Christ, redeeming a fallen creation, and God's salvation will ultimately
prevail over sin and evil.

The problem with the free will defense is that the more one thinks
about it in a common sense way, the less plausible it seems. Questions
abound. If this world was created as a paradise, then where did the impulse to rebel come from? "Oh, the mystery of freedom," we may say, but
that begs its own intellectual questions. It is sometimes right to play the
mystery card in theology, but here it looks evasive. At this point, I agree
with David Ray Griffin:

> Throughout most of Christian history in Europe (roughly the 4th
> to the 18th centuries), the cultural situation was such that the re-
> ality of God seemed overwhelmingly obvious to most people. . . .
> In such a situation the theologian could, when having trouble rec-
> onciling Christian doctrines with each other, appeal to "mystery"
> without defaulting on the theological task. Likewise, when Chris-

48. Ehrman, *God's Problem,* pp. 13-15.

78

tian doctrines conflicted with the conclusions of "reason," the theologian could simply appeal to authority (including the "authority" of reason which provided proofs for the existence of God), which supported the Christian doctrines. In other words, the theologian did not need to present a comprehensive view of the world that was *intrinsically convincing*. . . . The problem of evil in that situation constituted no overwhelming problem threatening to undermine faith itself. There was widespread confidence that there *was* a solution, known to God, and there was no overriding need to be able to discover that solution. Theologians often did devote many pages to it, but when they encountered questions they could not answer, there was no sense of desperation. They could calmly say that those remaining problems were "mysteries" which we were not intended to understand.

But in our day, all of this has changed.[49]

No way around it; if there was a rebellion in paradise, then there was disease there somewhere. If the world was perfect, then from whence did it come?

Also, how much sense does it make to trace all evil, moral and natural, to some act of rebellion in our common past? As far as natural science can tell, the conditions for volcanoes, hurricanes, and earthquakes have been in the world since the very beginning and are not the result of some sudden shift in geological (or theological) history. The idea of free will may explain some forms of evil and suffering. A car accident after a high school graduation party that claims four lives is certainly tragic, but we can see how free choices were involved. But what about the sheer scale of human suffering? All of those thousands of children and others killed in the Indian Ocean tsunami, or the millions destroyed in the holocaust. How much moral sense does it really make to blame their deaths on human beings choosing to abuse freedom or on a rebellion on the part of their human ancestors and of angels?

For most people today, the story of the "fall" in Genesis is less plausi-

49. David Ray Griffin, "Creation Out of Chaos and the Problem of Evil," in *Encountering Evil: Live Options in Theodicy*, ed. Stephen T. Davis (Atlanta: John Knox Press, 1981), p. 118.

ble as etiology — that is, as a description of what happened once upon a time that caused certain things to be (e.g., how it is that snakes came to crawl on their bellies instead of walking; how it came to be that sin entered the world) — and makes more sense as a mythological narrative depicting what is ever true of life and human experience. If sin is in the world, it is not because two historical figures, Adam and Eve, sinned at some point in time, and from that point onward a moral infection spread like smallpox among their descendants. It is rather that the story of Adam and Eve is the always repeated story of humanity. They are our representatives; we sin as they did because they are human beings, too, and we are like them. As Paul put it, "As was the man of dust [Adam], so are those who are of the dust . . ." (1 Cor. 15:48a).

The television evangelist Pat Robertson put forth a particularly odious example of the "free will" theodicy when he claimed that the January 2010 earthquake in Haiti had happened as a result of an evil choice on the part of Haitians two centuries earlier. In a revolution led by former slave François-Dominique Toussaint L'Ouverture and completed in 1804, Haitians successfully freed themselves from French colonial domination. Robertson generated a highly imaginative version of this episode in Haitian history when he said,

> They were under the heel of the French — you know, Napoleon the third and whatever [actually Napoleon Bonaparte]. And they got together and swore a pact to the devil. They said, "We will serve you if you will get us free from the prince." True story. And so the devil said, "OK, it's a deal." And they kicked the French out. The Haitians revolted and got themselves free. But ever since they have been cursed by one thing after another.[50]

Robertson's version is particularly stupid and morally corrupt, of course, but it simply underscores the plausibility problems that even more sophisticated versions of the free-will theodicy encounter — namely, that it makes little sense to people today to rest the blame for a hurricane, an earthquake, a mudslide, or any other natural disaster in

---

50. Pat Robertson on "The 700 Club," as reported by CBSnews.com, http://www .cbsnews.com/8301-504083_162-12017-504083.html.

the present on some otherwise unrelated moral misdeed earlier in human history.

An Irenaean Theodicy?

Theologian and philosopher John Hick, who has thoroughly explored Augustine's free-will position in his book *Evil and the God of Love*,[51] has proposed an alternative to the free-will view of theodicy. He claims to derive it from the writings of the early church pastor and theologian Irenaeus, but that claim has come under criticism.[52] As we have seen, the theodicy problem proper was an eighteenth-century development in theology and philosophy. Irenaeus, writing in the second and early third centuries, obviously knew nothing of this problem in its modern form. (The same can be said of Augustine, of course, and his "free will" description is not at all a modern theodicy — namely, a defense of belief in God — but instead an explanation of how humanity got bound up with evil and found itself in need of the redemption of Christ.) For theologians like Augustine and Irenaeus, claims Kenneth Surin, "little or no scope is allowed for any of the metaphysical or ontological stratagems that are inexplicably bound up with the typically modern enterprise of theodicy."[53]

But when Hick looks to Irenaeus for help on theodicy, he is simply doing what all theologians do, to one degree or another, when they turn

---

51. John Hick, *Evil and the God of Love*, rev. ed. (San Francisco: Harper & Row, 1978).

52. One shortcoming of Hick's Irenaean theodicy is that Hick himself no longer finds it compelling. After Hick wrote *Evil and the God of Love*, his own theology migrated away from the idea of a God who is a being carrying out intentions through time and toward a more global understanding of religions as but purely human images crafted in response to Ultimate Reality, or "The Real," about which almost nothing certain can be said. As a consequence of this theological shift, Hick has said some contradictory things about his Irenaean theodicy. On the one hand, he has implied that it no longer can be trusted as a description of what is actually happening in human experience, but, on the other hand, it is still a mythological formulation that provokes a Christian response to the reality of evil. As such, the Irenaean theodicy is, among Christian theodicies, still the most viable. See the discussion of this in John Hick, "An Irenaean Theodicy," in *Encounters with Evil*, new ed., ed. Davis, esp. pp. 52-72.

53. Surin, *Theology and the Problem of Evil*, p. 10.

to ancient sources for insight on current questions. To be sure, Irenaeus did not have theodicy on the radar screen; his theological writing was occupied with combatting the rising tide of Gnosticism in the church and with other pastoral concerns. What Hick has done is to tease thoughts and themes from these writings and to piece them together into a response to the contemporary problem of theodicy. The result, critics complain, is at least as much Hick as it is Irenaeus. Hick's so-called Irenaean theodicy is, however, an intriguing approach to the problem, and, leaving matters of provenance aside, it is worthy of exploration on merit alone.

Augustine, as we have seen, imagined that God created a paradise — not too hot, not too cold, but just right. But what, asks Hick, if this harmoniously balanced environment is *our* idea of paradise and not God's? What if God's ideal creation is not some perpetual Caribbean vacation, but instead a more rugged and demanding environment, a setting in which human beings can change and flourish, a milieu in which souls are made? As Irenaeus famously said, "The glory of God is humanity fully alive." So, what if God's goal for each of us is not to relax in some hothouse of perpetual pleasure but instead to grow and mature to the point that we are fully alive in God? What kind of world would God have created?

God would not have fashioned Augustine's paradise, but instead God would have created a world in which two conditions prevail: humanity would be "epistemically distant" from God, and God would be hidden from humanity. To put this in more classical terms, humanity would not have been created perfect, only to fall from perfection in the Garden of Eden. Instead, humanity would have been created full of potential, but immature, needing to travel some distance toward God and toward full humanity. And in this pilgrimage toward fullness, God must remain somewhat hidden, because a full manifestation of God's presence would bowl us over and prevent any meaningful human choice and exercise of freedom.[54]

When my daughter was a little girl and was in her doll-playing phase, we gave her many dolls, most of the early ones rag dolls and plastic dolls, all with beautiful, fixed smiles on their faces. But at one point — for a

54. Hick, *Evil and the God of Love*, pp. 281, 287.

birthday or Christmas, I can't remember — she asked for a doll that cried and wet its pants. As her father, I was completely puzzled by this. "She wants a doll that cries and wets its pants?" I asked my wife. "Why not stick with the dolls that smile all the time? Why does she want *trouble*?" The reason she wanted "trouble," of course, was that there was developing in her a desire to mother a real child, and she wanted one that needed her. She wanted one that would not already be in some frozen state of bliss, but one that would desire her, choose to love her, and grow toward her.

So, what if God is the same way? What if God wants us to freely choose to respond to God's love for us and to grow toward God? Then what kind of world would God create; what kind of world would "paradise" be? Perhaps the very world that we have. Perhaps this world, full of risk and joy, suffering and wonder, the world in which God is present but hidden from view, is the very best of all worlds for "soul-making."

It is inevitable that humanity would start off egocentric and curved in on itself. God is hidden and distant; what else could humanity be? Sin, in other words, is not a mysterious accident that happens in Paradise, but a necessary precondition for soul-making. Perhaps more radically, in a world of soul-making, it is necessary that, at the beginning, the world seems to humanity as if there were no God.[55] But humanity feels the loving invitation of a mystery beyond itself, calling it to grow and mature. The humanity that struggles toward perfection is better than some notion of humanity created perfect right out of the box. And it is God's patient intention that all humanity will grow to oneness with God. Hick quotes what Julian of Norwich heard the voice of Jesus say to her: "Sin must needs be, but all shall be well. All shall be well; and all manner of thing shall be well."[56]

This "Irenaean" response to theodicy gets us somewhere. It rings true to our experience, to the faithful intuition that whatever response we are going to be able to make to evil and suffering in the world, that response will not come in a logical formula but out of the actual experi-

---

55. Hick, *Evil and the God of Love*, p. 281.

56. Julian of Norwich, *The Revelations of Divine Love of Julian of Norwich* (London: Burns & Oates, 1961), chap. 27, as quoted in Hick, *Evil and the God of Love*, p. 289.

ence of struggle. It recognizes that the Christian faith is, indeed, a kind of pilgrimage of soul-making, putting one foot in front of the other on an often wearing and painful path, toward eschatological hope that one day "all will be well, all manner of things will be well." The Irenaean theodicy has a resonance with the hymn "Amazing Grace":

> Through many dangers, toils and snares
> we have already come.
> 'Twas grace that brought us safe thus far,
> and grace will lead us home.

Or, even more graphically, it finds expression in the words of the hymn that has been called the Black National Anthem, "Lift Every Voice and Sing":

> Stony the road we trod, bitter the chastening rod,
> Felt in the days when hope unborn had died;
> Yet with a steady beat, have not our weary feet,
> Come to the place for which our fathers sighed?
> We have come over a way that with tears has been watered,
> We have come, treading our path through the blood of the
>   slaughtered;
> Out from the gloomy past, till now we stand at last
> Where the white gleam of our bright star is cast.

But, as compelling as the Irenaean approach may be, there are problems here, too. The first is that this soul-making theodicy runs aground on the shoals of catastrophic and absurd evil. Some forms of evil and suffering are so massive, so irrational, so lacking in any possible redemptive value, that it is impossible to see any soul-making function at work.[57] Six

57. Marilyn McCord Adams has perceptively raised the special problem of catastrophic evil in *Horrendous Evils and the Goodness of God* (Ithaca, N.Y.: Cornell University Press, 1999). She defines "horrendous evil" as "evils the participation in which . . . constitutes prima facie reason to doubt whether the participant's life . . . could be a great good to him/her on the whole" — in other words, evil that clearly has no possible benefit to a person. In Adams's view, calling God "good" would demand that God defeat horrendous evil by guaranteeing a positive meaning that outweighs the evil *"within the context of his or her life"* (p. 31, emphasis in the original).

million Jews destroyed in the Holocaust; a five-year-old girl repeatedly raped by her father and then murdered . . . whose soul gets made by that? Some forms of evil are absurd, beyond any rational ability to find redemptive purpose in them. Hick is aware of this problem, and basically just throws up his hands and says, "It's a mystery." He writes,

> Our "solution," then, to this baffling problem of excessive and undeserved suffering is a frank appeal to the positive value of mystery. Such suffering remains unjust and inexplicable, haphazard and cruelly excessive . . . a real mystery, impenetrable to the rationalizing human mind. It challenges Christian faith with its utterly baffling, alien, and destructive meaninglessness. And yet at the same time, detached theological reflection can note that this very irrationality and this lack of ethical meaning contribute to the character of the world as a place in which true human goodness can occur and in which loving sympathy and compassionate self-sacrifice can take place. "Thus paradoxically," as H. H. Farmer says, "the failure of theism to solve all mysteries becomes part of its case."[58]

Not for most thinking Christians it doesn't. To say at the beginning of the discussion that "it's a mystery" how catastrophic evil is a part of a soul-making world, but that we trust that it is, fails the ethical test we set out at the beginning. Can we say to the father whose whole family was lost in the tsunami, "Well, this tsunami was a tragedy, absurd and meaningless suffering, but when you think about it from the viewpoint of detached theological reflection, we affirm that this very irrationality and this lack of ethical meaning contribute to the character of the world as a place in which true human goodness can occur"? I think not.

An equally powerful objection to this Irenaean theodicy is found not in absurd evil, but in the evil and suffering that perhaps could be forced into making sense. This scheme makes God, in a way, the author of evil. At least, if the way to full humanity is to be a soul-making odyssey, then the path will be necessarily littered with suffering and evil. Suffering is a required precondition for soul-making, and the way God created the

---

58. Hick, *Evil and the God of Love*, pp. 335-36.

world. Evil and suffering work in the total process toward gaining the higher good.

It was Dostoevsky who most magnificently raised an objection to this in *The Brothers Karamazov*. Ivan and Alyosha are arguing about the issue of evil, and Ivan tells one terrible tale after another — of soldiers who toss babies in the air only to impale them on bayonets; of a child who accidentally injures an army officer's dog and in punishment is stripped and made to run while a pack of hounds is set on him, tearing him to pieces; of a little girl tortured by her parents, made to sleep at night in a freezing outhouse, praying in vain all night "Dear God" with "unredeemed tears."

Then Ivan says that he knows the promise of heaven, the promise that one day all creation will be in harmony. He can imagine a day when the mother of the child torn apart by dogs will embrace the torturer in love and forgiveness, and the child himself will forgive, and the whole universe will tremble when heaven and earth merge, and all will see how everything works together for good and will cry out in praise, "Just art Thou, O God, thy ways are revealed." Ivan says he knows this promise, but if the cost of a ticket to this heaven is one of these children being tortured, then the price of harmony is too high. "It's not that I don't accept God, Alyosha, I just most respectfully return him the ticket."[59]

David Bentley Hart has rightly seen Ivan's (and Dostoevsky's) response not as doubting or faithless, but as deeply Christian. When one looks at the actual suffering in the world, not suffering as a hypothetical problem, but the actual suffering, then no theology that includes this suffering as a God-given part of a creation made for soul-making can claim to be Christian, even with a beautifully harmonious eschatology attached. A God who requires or allows a child to be tortured as a necessary part of redeeming the world is the author of evil and a moral monster. Such a view of evil and God is not like a parent saying to a child before emergency surgery, "This may be painful, but it is to save your life, and you will understand it one day." It is like a parent placing a hot iron on the face of a child and saying, "You will understand this someday." No "someday" can fully account for such an act, and a God

---

59. Fyodor Dostoevsky, *The Brothers Karamazov* (New York: Farrar, Straus & Giroux, 2002), p. 245.

who parents like that cannot be trusted. More specifically, such a God is not the one revealed in Jesus Christ. As Lewis Smedes (whom we mentioned in Chapter 2) said, he did not believe, nor did he desire, that there would come some fine day when God would make the death of his newborn son all plain and clear, so that Smedes, now understanding why this was somehow necessary, would then be able to praise God that it had happened. Hart writes, "Voltaire [the Deist] sees only the terrible truth that the history of suffering and death is not morally intelligible. Dostoevsky [the Christian] sees . . . that it would be far more terrible if it were."[60]

What Gives?

If many thoughtful Christians today would pose the theodicy question as some version of the impossible chess match in which at least one of four theological claims must give way, what have we learned from this survey of options for theodicy? Which claim should yield?

There is a God.
God is all-powerful.
God is loving and good.
There is innocent suffering.

Having explored the thought of fellow pilgrims, the best response, I would argue, is "all of the above." All four of the claims are transformed by the Christian gospel. Each of the theodicies portrayed here, like the old story of the blind men trying to describe an elephant, has gotten hold of a piece of the truth. When we take them together, we can see how, for Christians, each of the four terms of the impossible chess match requires modification and re-description. Let me briefly sketch what I mean.

First, there is the question of God. The classical theodicy problem, as defined in the eighteenth century, conceived of God essentially as a large

---

60. David Bentley Hart, *The Doors of the Sea: Where Was God in the Tsunami?* (Grand Rapids: Wm. B. Eerdmans, 2005), p. 44.

source of willful energy outside of nature (i.e., the supernatural). If God so willed, that energy could be exerted from the outside into the natural system to change the course of events. It was almost as if God were a super-powerful spectator at a football game. If the halfback broke through the line and were streaking for a touchdown and this displeased God, God could reach into the game, knock the halfback down, and prevent the touchdown. So when the "halfback" is the Lisbon earthquake, why didn't God reach in?

Christians, however, do not think of God in such supernaturalistic ways, do not think of God as some energy force outside of the natural order. The process theologians, and to some extent Kushner, help us to reject this unbiblical view of God. In most Christian theology, there is care taken to maintain a delicate balance in describing the relationship between God and the "natural" world, the creation. On the one hand, God and the creation are not one and the same, and God is not merely the sum of all the life-giving processes at work in nature (pantheism). On the other hand, God and the creation are not totally separate and independent entities. For Christianity, God — the God narrated in Scripture — is involved in creation, in nature, but is not completely contained in creation. In fact, Christianity speaks not only of God "in" the world or God "apart from" the world, but also of the whole creation "in" God.

When a young survivor of the Haiti earthquake said, "We have survived by the grace of God," and Haitian bishop Éric Toussaint, standing near the damaged cathedral, said, "We are in the hands of God now," *New Yorker* writer and Harvard literary critic James Wood was empathetic but finally scornful of these references to the deity. Such responses to tragedy are, he wrote, "entirely understandable, uttered in a ruined landscape beyond the experience of most of us, and a likely source of pastoral comfort to the bishop's desperate flock. But that should not obscure the fact that it is little more than a piece of helpless mystification, a contradictory cry of optimistic despair."[61] Op-ed writer Robert Reyes was even more dismissive of what he called "illogical religion-inspired lunacy." The earthquake survivors in Haiti, he said,

---

61. James Wood, "Between God and a Hard Place," *New York Times*, 24 January 2010, WK11.

... aren't in the hands of God (not a very safe place to be), but in the hands of their powerful neighbor, the United States. Their salvation lies not in the Almighty, but in the American ships and planes that are bringing in desperately needed food, water, building materials, and medical supplies.[62]

But both Woods and Reyes are trapped by a definition of God that comes from philosophy and from Deism, but is unknown to Trinitarian faith. If by "the grace of God" and "the hands of God," these Haitians were referring to the external, supernatural God of philosophical theism, the God outside of creation, the God in the stadium skybox who could have reached in to knock down the halfback and change the game, then the critics were right to be disdainful, right to claim that a disaster like the devastation in Haiti pushes up toward agnosticism or atheism, right to look to more human and political sources of redemption. But if these Haitian Christians are, rather, referring to the God of Jesus Christ, the God who became flesh and dwelled among us, the God of Elijah's "still small voice," then this is, indeed, another God altogether, one about whom it is fitting to speak of God's grace and care in the midst of suffering. They would be speaking of God's involvement in their suffering in the same language used by a patient in an AIDS hospice, who prayed,

> Father, I am calling out to you.
> Bless each patient name by name;
> These are your children.
> Lord, bless their families,
> And those who do not know
> You are in this.
> Go in, Lord, and touch 'em.
> Hallelujah!

Second, there is the question of God's power. Although Kushner and the process theologians went too far in delimiting divine power, they were right to realize that the God we see in the light of Jesus Christ is a

62. Robert Paul Reyes, "Religious Lunacy: Haitian Rev. Eric Toussaint, 'Give Thanks to God,'" *News Blaze,* 10 January 2010; http://newsblaze.com/story/20100117110433reye .nb/topstory.html.

God who exercises power in unconventional ways. Douglas John Hall says, "Every responsible attempt to rethink the question of 'God and human suffering' . . . must involve in a primary sense a radical reinterpretation of divine omnipotence."[63] If we think of God's power in the same way that we conceive of worldly power, in the way we think of a powerful ruler or a powerful army, we have, says Hall, rendered unto God the things that belong to Caesar![64]

Third, there is the goodness and love of God. The thinkers we have examined have, all in their own ways, placed a premium on this claim. The last thing any of them are willing to forfeit is the affirmation of God's love. It is an interesting and revealing statement about our age that some of them would even be willing to jettison the idea of God altogether before yielding an inch on divine loving-kindness. Here and there, though, these theologians have been willing to admit that, when it comes to theodicy and we start talking about God's love, justice, and goodness, it usually turns out that what we mean is *our* sense of love, justice, and goodness, projected large onto God. We say, "Well, *I* wouldn't have created a world with mosquitoes bearing the West Nile virus, and *I'm* a good and loving person; why would a good and loving God allow such a thing?" To do this, of course, imposes upon God as ethical demands constructions of "goodness" and "love" crafted out of the values of the cultural moment. "Why do you call me good?" Jesus shockingly responded to the rich ruler. "No one is good — except God alone" (Luke 18:19). Whatever else that enigmatic verse may mean, it implies that "good" is a virtue that gets defined by the character of God and not the other way around.

Finally, there is the experience of innocent suffering, which most contemporary discussions of theodicy take as axiomatic. We know what we're getting at here. When a drunk driver roars through a stop sign and hits a child on a bicycle coming home from school, killing her instantly, we call the child an "innocent victim." She did nothing to deserve the loss of her life. She may have made the choice to be riding her bike across that particular intersection at that particular time, but these choices do not implicate her morally in the evil event that occurred. She is without

63. Hall, *God and Human Suffering*, p. 155.
64. Hall, *God and Human Suffering*, p. 155.

blame. Any court, on earth or in heaven, would find her innocent of any act that caused her death.

But there is a second meaning of *innocent,* one which may render it not the best word to use. *Innocent,* as we have seen, can mean "morally blameless," but it can also mean "utterly lacking" in something, as in "He was utterly innocent of any knowledge of calculus" or "Her manner was utterly innocent of trickery." To call the child on the bike "innocent" in this sense would be to say that she was utterly lacking in anything at all that should have put her in harm's way. What this would do is remove her from the rough-and-tumble, the risks and dangers of ordinary life and put her into a special, sterile category of the "innocent," as if she had been struck down not by another human being driving through the same intersection but by a dart shot by Satan or by a raw energy wave flung toward earth from another universe.

In this sense, rather than speaking of her death as "innocent," it would be more fitting to call it "tragic." What this change in terminology does is make it clear that the child's death, though certainly out of joint with what human life should be, is thoroughly consistent with what human life, in fact, is. She may be innocent of moral blame, but she is not innocent of being a human being, with all the perils and possibilities inherent in that condition. She suffered, and those who loved her suffered, but not because of anything she did wrong; their suffering is evidence that they are human and full participants in human experience. This use of *tragic* rather than *innocent* also preserves us from finally being more outraged at her death than had she been, say, a teenage boy fleeing on a bicycle from just having stolen a purse. We might be tempted to say, "Well, it's sad he was killed, but he had just committed a theft. In a way, he deserved it. But she was just an innocent child." However, as William Munny, the Clint Eastwood character in the Western movie *Unforgiven* says, "Deserve's got nothing to do with it." The intoxicated driver barreling through the intersection, the chance intersection of car and bicycle, were oblivious to the moral character of the bicyclist. It was, however we look at it, a tragic event.

So, WE HAVE SEEN THAT "the impossible chess match" has some flex in each of its major terms. But we are still short of describing what a preacher can say to a congregation of thoughtful Christians troubled and challenged by theodicy. To that compelling question we must now turn, but not before pausing to explore the biblical example of suffering *par excellence,* the sufferer to which virtually everyone concerned about theodicy turns: Job.

INTERLUDE

Howl: Job and the Whirlwind

The Joban drama is perhaps the longest-running story in the history of human experience. The biblical Job is but one, if one of the best, of a cast of characters who has played this role.

Samuel E. Balentine, *Job*[1]

I saw the best minds of my generation destroyed by
    madness, . . .
angelheaded hipsters burning for the ancient heavenly
    connection to the starry dynamo in the machinery
    of night.

Allen Ginsberg, "Howl"[2]

S ooner or later, most people who ponder the question of faith and innocent suffering turn to the biblical book of Job. If Jesus is the most

---

1. Samuel E. Balentine, *Job* (Macon, Ga.: Smith and Helwys, 2006), pp. 4-5.
2. Allen Ginsberg, *"Howl" and Other Poems* (San Francisco: City Lights Publishers, 2001), p. 9.

significant sufferer in the Christian Scriptures, then Job is surely the most humanly recognizable one. In his story of anguished suffering and troubled faith, symbolically Job is neither Jew nor Greek, male nor female, ancient nor modern. Job is from the land of Uz, a place no one can find on a map but a place where nearly everyone has spent some time. Job is every person, transcending particularity of time and place.

One of the most intriguing aspects of the book of Job, however, is how devilishly difficult it is to tell what the book is about. "You have heard of the patience of Job," remarks the Epistle of James, and indeed we have. Anyone who is satisfied, however, that this little slogan adequately summarizes the book has evidently grown weary after reading only the first two chapters. Stephen Mitchell's exciting translation of the story has Job breaking his silence at the beginning of chapter three with the words "God damn the day I was born"[3] — the words of a man whose patience, if he ever had any, has clearly worn a bit thin.

Most of us know that patience was never really a serious contender as a summary meaning for Job, anyway. We are far more likely to see the book as a theological treatise on the question that has occupied our attention throughout this book: theodicy. Like Rabbi Kushner, many other readers of Scripture have turned to Job seeking wisdom on the question of why innocent people have to suffer in a world created by a good God. As one biblical scholar has said, "Among the biblical books that entail theodicy the Book of Job is one of the most important."[4]

But this understanding of Job as a treatise on theodicy is also problematic and ultimately disappointing. We do not get from the story what we expect or hope for. Rabbi Kushner, as we have seen, had to twist a passage from Job out of shape to make it yield an answer to his theodicy question. Most readers of Job, though, come to the end of the book and are simply confused by, or deeply dissatisfied with, even aggrieved by, the results. The God who finally turns up near the end of the story appears to supply not an answer but a swagger. God seems to thump the divine chest, demanding to know who this Job character thinks he is, anyway.

---

3. Stephen Mitchell, *The Book of Job* (San Francisco: North Point Press, 1987). Many of the quotations in this chapter from the book of Job are from Mitchell's translation.

4. Karl-Johan Illman, "Theodicy in Job," in *Theodicy in the World of the Bible*, ed. Antti Laato and Johannes C. de Moor (Leiden: Brill, 2003), p. 304.

Most teachers are aware that if a student asks an embarrassingly difficult question, one way to handle it is to raise your voice, act insulted, and make the student feel silly and presumptuous for having asked. Could it be that the God of the book of Job has learned this technique?

David Robertson thinks so. He draws our attention to Job's speech in chapter 9, in which Job predicts what would happen if he summoned God to a face-to-face encounter.[5] "If it is a contest of strength, behold him!" says Job. "Though I am innocent, my own mouth would condemn me." In short, Job predicts that, should God appear to him, he will be muscled aside by the divine power into inauthentic self-condemnation. Sure enough, claims Robertson, when God finally does appear, Job's prediction comes true:

> So God's rhetoric [in chapters 38–41], because Job has warned us
> against it, convinces us that he is a charlatan God, one who has
> the power and skill of God but is a fake at the truly divine task of
> governing with justice and love.[6]

Terrence Tilley suggests that it is no wonder that people who go to Job looking for explanations about why innocent people suffer end up disappointed. Job is not a theodicy, he argues, but a kind of anti-theodicy. The purpose of the text is to overthrow our desire to know why suffering happens. It is Job's friends, after all, the villains of the piece, who try to "do" theodicy, who attempt to craft explanations for Job's suffering and to defend the honor of God. The fact that Job is about the failure of theodicy is the reason, Tilley argues, that many of the philosophical theodicists instinctively avoid the book of Job altogether. Seeing their own pomposity and ignorance reflected in the shallow approach of Job's so-called comforters, "theodicists typically neither interpret nor repeat nor reject Job. They ignore the text and silence Job's voice."[7]

Philosopher and theologian David B. Burrell agrees. In his revealingly titled book about Job, *Deconstructing Theodicy: Why Job Has Noth-*

5. David Robertson, "The Book of Job: A Literary Study," *Soundings* 56 (1973): 446-69.

6. Robertson, "The Book of Job," p. 464.

7. Terrence W. Tilley, *The Evils of Theodicy* (Eugene, Ore.: Wipf & Stock, 2000), p. 89.

ing to Say to the Puzzle of Suffering, Burrell maintains that a principal function of Job is to deconstruct all of the "sober efforts of philosophers to construct theories" that defend the character of God.[8]

Despite Tilley's and Burrell's attempts to wave us off, however, no Christian asking about innocent suffering can finally stay away from this compelling story. The book of Job is an enormously subtle and complex work, amenable to multiple readings, and there is still at least one more possibility for understanding its central subject matter worth pursuing, one that can finally have profound implications for preaching on theodicy — namely, Job's suffering is an urgent test case in the larger issue of humanity's relationship with God. The book of Job, therefore, is not devoted to explaining philosophically how a good God and innocent suffering can occupy the same space; it is instead about who God is and what it means to be *human at all* when God is understood truly to be God. This great text stands over against the prevalent religious impulse to fabricate a wishful picture of the world, to imagine the sort of God who would rule benignly over such a world, and then to bow down in worship before this projection of our own sense of moral order.

Because Job suffers so grievously and so irrationally, he is no longer permitted the luxury of an illusion. Every attempt at make-believe falls before the reality of empty places at his family table and the throbbing pain in his body. The only god Job can manufacture from his misery is a monster, and Job must decide whether to flee from this arbitrary and punitive god or to stand up boldly to see if there just might be another — a God not of his own making. Stephen Mitchell observed that William Blake, who created a series of engravings on Job, "is still the only interpreter to understand that the theme of this book is spiritual transformation."[9] Perhaps Blake is among the few to see in Job what is involved in coming to live before the only God we cannot construct.

---

8. David B. Burrell, *Deconstructing Theodicy: Why Job Has Nothing to Say to the Puzzle of Suffering* (Grand Rapids: Brazos Press, 2008), p. 107.

9. Mitchell, *The Book of Job,* p. xxix.

Job: The Stage Play

In order to see how this issue of spiritual transformation is developed, let us look at the book itself. In some ways this is easier said than done, since it is not entirely clear what we are looking *at*. Part folktale, part epic poem, part dialogue, Job is a jumble of genres, and historical critics are quick to point out that the present form seems to have resulted from the work of a rather heavy set of editorial hands. Taken as a whole, however, Job seems more like an elaborately staged *play* than anything else. As Luis Alonso Schökel has observed, reading Job as a drama appears to offer the best chance to view the entire work as we have it as "intelligible and comprehensible in its unity."[10]

The curtain opens to reveal the land of Uz. We *see* Uz, but we *hear* the voice of an unseen narrator: "There was a man in the land of Uz whose name was Job . . ." Efforts to locate Uz on the map are in vain, for this is not a historical chronicle. The narrative effect of the opening lines, like the opening credits of the movie *Star Wars,* is to say that this is a story that happened "long ago and far away."[11] As the narrator speaks, the stage is gradually filled by the clan of Job, and the whole scene has a dream-like perfection. Job is "the richest man in the East" and possesses "perfect integrity." He "feared God and avoided evil." Job not only has sons, daughters, and animals, he has them in symmetrical numbers: seven sons, three daughters, seven thousand sheep, three thousand camels, five hundred oxen, and five hundred donkeys.[12] There is something a bit *too* perfect about all this, of course: Job is like a man in a silk hat and a tuxedo walking down a snow-covered street. It's only a matter of time before the snowballs begin to fly. Here at the very outset, the audience begins to sense what will become even more apparent later: they are watching not only a play but a "profoundly serious" *comedy.*[13]

To this point, at least, the drama is a "tall tale," employing the classic

10. Luis Alonso Schökel, "Toward a Dramatic Reading of the Book of Job," *Semeia* 7 (1977): 46.

11. J. Gerald Janzen, *Job,* Interpretation Commentaries (Atlanta: John Knox Press, 1985), p. 34.

12. William Whedbee, "The Comedy of Job," *Semeia* 7 (1977): 5.

13. Whedbee, "The Comedy of Job," p. 4.

comedic technique of exaggeration. Like Paul Bunyan, Job is the tallest and the strongest and the best, and thus does not evoke an existential connection with the plight of the human beings in the audience. He stands at some distance from the ordinary round of human life. At this point, Job is not "everyman"; he is "superman." And the audience waits either for yet another tale of his unvanquished power — or for the banana peel that will send him reeling.

The flawlessness of Job's life in Uz extends to the moral realm. The narrator tells us that every year Job's sons hold a gala family "progressive dinner," moving from house to house. This annual time of feasting would prompt Job to demand that his children submit to a ritual of purification, not because he knew they had done anything wrong, mind you, but because they *might,* in the midst of all this merriment, have harbored a sinful thought. This is a super-scrupulous Job, the "perfect moral businessman" who knows how to succeed at the reward game, in life and with God. But Job's world is inherently unstable, since the slightest transgression, the faintest crack in the moral surface, could bring it down, leading to moral and fiscal bankruptcy.[14] Thus, Job is forced to live, as Calvin Trillin, in another context, wryly observed, in "the Era of Year-Round Yom Kippur."[15]

Suddenly, the stage lighting shifts, and the audience views not Uz but the heavenly court. God is there. The angels are there. And, on this occasion, the Adversary is there also. The Adversary reports that he has been occupying his time "going to and fro on the earth," and, in a line that has to be interpreted as a throwing down of some kind of gauntlet, God says, "Did you notice my servant Job?" What follows, of course, is the picking up of the gauntlet by the Adversary and the famous wager: "Take away everything Job has, and I'll bet even 'your servant' will curse you."

Back to Uz we go, and what happens is a scene of high tragi-comedy. Modern readers will miss the comic dimension unless we are willing to accept the deeply stylized character of the events. The actions are so hyperbolic that, while they serve to advance the plot, they cannot be taken

14. Mitchell, *The Book of Job,* p. 9.
15. Calvin Trillin, *Third Helpings* (New York: Penguin Books, 1983), p. 9.

as completely serious descriptions of what is possible in human life. They are, to borrow Mitchell's term, "puppet theater."[16] Wave upon wave of messengers arrive with news increasingly dire. They step all over each other's lines: "While he was yet speaking, there came another . . ." Sabeans have attacked; lightning has struck; Chaldeans have raided; everything — the children, the livestock, everything — has been lost. The world that had been *perfectly* wonderful now becomes *perfectly* miserable. This is like one of those old magazine insurance ads showing a suburban home undergoing simultaneous and multiple trauma: a windstorm is ripping off roof shingles, a baseball is passing through the picture window, and a burglar is jimmying the sliding glass door, while, at the same moment and at the same house, a workman is tumbling off a ladder, a tree is falling across the garage, and flames are licking through a side wall. Here, as in Job, more tragedy is taking place in the space of thirty seconds than occurs in the entire span of *King Lear*.

Astoundingly, and yet, in a way, predictably, Job continues to walk the upright line. Even when a second round of betting in the heavenly court ups the ante and brings actual physical suffering to Job himself, he remains firm. "We have accepted good fortune from God," Job explains to his wife. "Surely we can accept bad fortune, too."

It seems the Adversary has lost his bet. Nothing can shake God's servant Job. He stands there, banana peel on his shoe, silk hat askew and covered with snow, but unbowed, his "perfect integrity" intact. All that remains is for the narrator to "round out" the tale by telling us how the Adversary quit the wager in humiliation and defeat and how Job was rewarded for his steadfastness, riding off into the Gary Cooper kind of sunset prepared for those of his stature.

Indeed, it is widely held among Old Testament scholars that the original version of the story of Job ended precisely this way. The Adversary is embarrassed in the heavenly court, God wins the bet hands down, and Job has his fortunes restored — end of religious tall tale. If this truly is how the Job story once ended, then the original version was a theological "exemplary anecdote," an Aesop's fable with a moral tagline about the virtues of steadfastness. It's a sermon illustration, if you will.

16. Mitchell, *The Book of Job*, p. xii.

A Surplus of Tragic Meaning

Experienced preachers are aware, however, that sermon illustrations do not always work the way we intend. They have a life of their own. While the preachers think they are telling a clear and simple story about something like prayer or stewardship, the hearers are being taken by the story in another direction. There can be a "surplus of meaning" in a story, unfinished business. And some hearers resist the preachers' attempts to aim the story toward the intended target, remaining unsatisfied until this other dimension of the story has been resolved.

The original version of Job was such a story; and the author of the present version of Job was, evidently, such a hearer. Biblical scholar Samuel Balentine notes, "Taken as a set piece, this story, which many regard as the oldest part of the book, reads like an ancient version of a nineteenth-century Brothers Grimm fairy tale: 'Once upon a time' . . . and 'they all lived happily ever after,'" but the author of the present book of Job encountered this old fairy tale and "found the 'all's-well-that-ends-well' . . . story unsatisfying."[17]

The author of the *canonical* book of Job no doubt knew that the original plot of the story — perfect world/disaster/perfect world restored — was logically and existentially impossible. There was a surplus of meaning, a piece of unfinished business left unresolved by the original ending and intention. Job's "perfect world" was built upon the assumption that God plays by a set of moral rules that are widely publicized and known to humanity. As long as a person, like Job, obeys those rules, or engages in acts of purification when one of those rules may have inadvertently been broken, then God can be trusted to "play fair" and to preserve and protect. The problem, however, was that God broke the rules. The destruction and suffering experienced by Job came as the direct result of divine behavior, which, as far as the agreed-upon rules go, was definitely in foul territory. Job suffers not because he has violated some holy ordinance but because God played games with Job's life — issued a seemingly capricious challenge to an Adversary, made a wager in the heavenly court, and enigmatically turned Job over to the power of a malicious opponent. In short,

---

17. Balentine, *Job,* p. 14.

God's behavior broke the Humpty Dumpty world apart, and it makes no sense whatsoever to end the story by pretending that it could be put back together again. The plot of the story itself has destroyed the foundation upon which that world was built. The gates of Eden are blocked, and, wherever Job may go now, the one way he cannot go is back.

The author of the "revised" story of Job discerns the unfinished issue in the folktale and bravely leaves the confines of the old story in quest of a deeper resolution. The crucial question that demands working out is not why Job has suffered so, but what kind of God and what kind of creation allow for such a jagged piece of morally irrational experience. Job's suffering is not itself the question in focus, but the event that *raises* the crucial question of the character of God and the nature of humanity's relationship to God. In the theological economy of Job's former world, the suffering of a genuinely righteous person was mathematically impossible. But it happened. And because it happened, what is now "impossible" is Job's former world itself. So, the plot of the Job story lurches forward on a quest to discover the "new world," if there is one, or at least to answer the question, How do we live when our experience causes our theological universe to collapse?

The Anguished Dialogues

The author pursues this quest by way of a new linguistic style. The drama of Job shifts from the pattern of folktale to that of poetry and dialogue. An anguished, deeply perplexed, and outraged Job engages in conversation with three friends, a youthful bystander, and finally with God. The purpose of the dialogues is profoundly serious, but the author retains some of the comic motifs of the earlier narrative. In light of what the audience knows about Job's situation and God's involvement, many of the speeches of Job's companions border upon the absurd and are, at times, even laughable. They are also, ironically, often persuasive and beautiful. In constructing the speeches of the friends, the author "has acted with the instinctive generosity of all great poets, endowing the friends with a life and passion almost as intense as Job's."[18]

18. Mitchell, *The Book of Job,* p. xiv.

The basic design of this dialogical section involves Job's three friends giving three rounds of speeches, each speech generally followed by a reply from Job. Theatrically, this section is exhausting, since there is plenty of talk but no movement in the plot. The friends constantly repeat themselves, and each other, looping through the same arguments and scoring the same points over and over.[19] This lack of dramatic movement is not the product of authorial clumsiness; it is the very point of this section. Job's friends state and re-state their cases, and *nothing* happens. For all their efforts, the friends get us nowhere.

In the tiresome redundancy of their speeches, however, the audience does get to know the personalities and viewpoints of the friends. In effect, the friends become personifications of various non-answers to the crucial question of the drama. Indeed, if we will allow ourselves to listen to them and to become acquainted with them, we can recognize in them the familiar characters who even today hang around the church, stalling and sidetracking honest religious questing.

Eliphaz

This, the first of Job's friends, is the embodiment of a mushy brand of self-serving piety. "Job, will it bother you if I speak?" Eliphaz oozes in his opening line, just before attempting to shame Job for his lost faith. "Beware of people who go around talking about loving and caring," Walker Percy once warned.[20] Eliphaz is one of those folks who slithers up to people in anguish, his lips pursed with unctuous murmurs of concern while his pockets are lined with tracts spelling out the "spiritual laws." Eliphaz is the sort of person who begins his prayers with "Lord, I just want to ask . . ."; when you listen carefully, you realize that what he "just" wants to ask is that the Lord rearrange the entire material universe to suit his convenience.

Eliphaz surveys Job's situation and then gazes heavenward, telling

19. Robert Gordis, *The Book of God and Man: A Study of Job* (Chicago: University of Chicago Press, 1965), p. 4.

20. Walker Percy, *Lost in the Cosmos: The Last Self-Help Book* (New York: Farrar, Straus & Giroux, 1983), p. 187.

himself and Job that it is all an illusion. "Sin has seduced your mind," he intones. "You are lucky that God has scolded you," he soothes. His advice? "If I were you, I would pray. . . . Make peace with God; you will not be sorry." The result? "Everything you do will succeed and light will shine on your path." The maddening thing about Eliphaz is that he has turned some of faith's strongest affirmations into cross-stitched slogans suitable for hanging on the wall. For Eliphaz, the power of prayer is a bargaining chip, peace with God a negotiating device. He does not have faith; he has a religion machine.

Eliphaz's response to the question "How do we live when our experience causes our theological universe to collapse?" is to deny our experience. His system of piety allows him to manipulate the strings of divine providence, and any experience that challenges those pious formulations must be quickly filtered out as a threat. Eliphaz is so busy painting the "Get Back to God" sign beside the old road that he has failed to notice that a new highway has been built and the old road abandoned.

Bildad

The second of Job's companions is a religious authoritarian. He has a bumper sticker on his car that reads, "God said it, I believe it, and that's that." Bildad views human nature as a bowl of spoiled mayonnaise, describing humanity as "that worm, that vile, stinking maggot." He has never been there himself, but Bildad can confidently tell us what goes on in college dormitories, denominational headquarters, the house next door, and every other cesspool of iniquity, because the man *knows* human nature and can sniff its foul odor through closed doors. Bildad is convinced that horrors, like AIDS and earthquakes, are well-deserved punishments for transgression, and what's more, such devastation makes him feel justified, even glad. "It is true," he proclaims with a casual shrug of his shoulders, "the sinner is snuffed out. . . . This is what happens to the godless."

It is no surprise, then, to hear Bildad telling Job, "Your children must have sinned against God, and so he punished them as they deserved." As for Job himself, "If you are pure and righteous," Bildad informs him, per-

WHAT SHALL WE SAY?

haps sarcastically, "and pray to God for mercy, surely he will answer your prayer." As the audience hears Bildad speak, their response will doubtless be a mixture of irritation and mirth. Bildad stands there like an iron rod, his shoes spit-shined and every hair carefully combed, insisting that it never rains on the righteous, even while his neatly pressed suit is getting drenched by the downpour.

Zophar

Zophar is a Bildad who has gone to seminary. He shares Bildad's rigid view of sin and punishment, but has learned to intellectualize it. Zophar sucks on his pipe and tells Job, who is at the moment scratching a boil with a piece of pottery, that this whole matter is complex, very complex, and that "there are many sides to wisdom." Zophar has decided that Job's whole problem is a lack of clarity: Job doesn't *understand* that he is a sinner. Zophar slaps his forehead, wondering, "Job, how can you be so blind?" He lectures Job on the doctrine of evil, but he is pessimistic about Job's chances to pass the class. "A stupid man will be wise," he quips, "when a cow gives birth to a zebra."

The audience knows, of course, that Zophar, for all his dissection of the pertinent issues, has also missed the point: in the economy of the story, Job is a truly righteous man. What is more important, the audience knows something the erudite Zophar does not know: Job's plight has been caused by a bet in heaven and not by some as-yet-undisclosed tragic flaw.

The speeches of Job in response to his friends are at times moving, occasionally hilarious, and always passionate and wildly beautiful. He fluctuates between bitterly opposing his friends and agreeing with them, if only sarcastically: "Yes, you are the voice of the people. When you die, wisdom will die with you." What he says to them is fascinating and revealing. He acknowledges that he used to believe and say everything they are claiming, but his experience no longer permits this. Job was the model of orthodoxy; he could spout proverbs with the best of them. But his own experience of innocent suffering is the one situation that this orthodoxy could not have anticipated and that its worldview cannot contain. Job admits that he was once a constant winner in the game of "Proverbs," but undeserved suffering turned out to be an unexpected Joker in the orthodox deck. Now that Job has drawn this card, he can no longer play his hand. The rules have changed; the game has changed.

For the Love of God

Even as Job addresses his friends, his speech spills over the bounds of human conversation. Job is talking to his friends, but also beyond them. He is not exactly speaking to God, but rather to the empty space which God may choose to fill. "I want to speak before God," he cries, "to present my case in God's court." He hurls into the Void a mockery of Psalm 8: "What is man, that you notice him, turn your glare upon him?" He shakes his fist at God, and then unfolds his fingers and begs for God's embrace. He knows he cannot return to the safe harbor of his former life, so he turns to face the storm. "I am ready to risk my life," he cries, his own howl now shouted into the howling wind. "So what if God kills me? I'm going to state my case to him. It may even be that my boldness will save me."

As we witness this drama, it gradually dawns upon us that what separates Job from his friends is that Job loves God. His friends love the religious system, but Job loves God. Unlike them, Job is willing, if he must, to give up his theology, but he will not give up his God. In the dark terror of his nightmare, Job cries out to the One who must surely be as close as the next room, "You would call me — I would answer; you would come to me and rejoice, delighting in my smallest step like a father watching his child." As Mitchell says:

> All this bewilderment and outrage couldn't be so intense if Job didn't truly love God. He senses that in spite of appearances there is somewhere an ultimate justice, but he doesn't know where. He is like a nobler Othello who has been brought conclusive evidence that his wife has betrayed him: his honesty won't allow him to disbelieve it, but his love won't allow him to believe it.[21]

21. Mitchell, *The Book of Job*, p. xvii.

As Job's words become more and more directed to the absent God, the friends become less and less pertinent to the drama. Everything is gathering itself for the inevitable divine appearance. But the author of Job has yet one more comedic surprise to spring. Job begs for the dark side of the stage to be filled with the light of God's presence. A timpani begins to roll in the orchestra pit. The string section vibrates excitedly. All eyes are directed with expectation toward the darkness. Suddenly, a spotlight snaps on, and there bathed in its light is . . . Elihu.

A sigh of disappointment goes up from the audience, and it is well-placed. Elihu is cradling his latest-generation smartphone, and his designer jeans are so fashionably faded that they hide the fact that they come from Nordstrom's. His beard is a failed attempt to disguise his youth. He knows this, and so he begins, "I am young and you are old, so I was afraid to tell you what I think, but now that these three so-called sages have utterly failed, someone from my generation is just going to have to step in to straighten out this mess."

Mustering all possible authority, Elihu continues, "I will not take sides in this debate; I am not going to flatter anyone. . . . All my words are sincere, and I am speaking the truth." It takes him six windy chapters to speak this truth, and when all is said and done, Elihu has mostly repeated the same theological mello-bits we have already heard from the three friends. They are spoken, however, with all the self-congratulation of a person who has stumbled across a well-worn truism and believes that he is its first discoverer. Elihu is all windup and no pitch. As William Whedbee says, "Though there may be 'no fool like an old fool,' Elihu, as a young fool, comes close."[22]

Out of the Whirlwind

After this false dénouement, then, the drama moves to its proper climax: the voice of God speaking out of the whirlwind. It is God's voice that is

---

22. Whedbee, "The Comedy of Job," p. 20. For a much more positive assessment of Elihu, see Carol A. Newsom, *The Book of Job: A Contest of Moral Imaginations* (New York: Oxford University Press, 2003), pp. 200ff.

described, but the images are so powerful that Job *sees* God acting across the expanse of eternity as much as he hears God speaking in the moment. "Where were you when I planned the earth?" challenges God. "Do you know who took its dimensions, measuring its length with a cord?" "Where were you when I stopped the waters?" "Is the wild ox willing to serve you? Do you deck the ostrich with wings?"

Job is awestruck: "I am speechless: what can I answer? I have said too much already."

God is not finished, however: "Stand up now like a human being. I have more to say." What God says, taken as rational discourse, reduces, as Mitchell has observed (and Kushner missed), to something like, "How dare you question the creator of the world? Shut up now, and submit." And if this is the proper summation of the divine speech, then Job's response becomes, "Yes, sir, Boss. Anything you say."[23] But God's speech is *not* rational discourse; it is poetic, visionary address, and as such it gathers us up into an experiential encounter that resists all reduction, all explanation.

Job's former world was a world of order, and this very order is what made talk of justice possible. Ideas of "right" and "wrong" were the rules of this ordered world, and Job understood God to be both the original rulemaker and the divine rulekeeper, the cosmic "umpire." But the unthinkable has happened. The umpire has violated the rules and, in Job's tormented view, has been unjust. Now the Voice from the whirlwind speaks, and it says that Job's system of order and rules was never God's to begin with. It was a human scheme of justice, projected from earth onto heaven. Job's cry of injustice turns out, at root, to be an attempt to impose the human notion of moral order upon God. In E. M. Good's translation of a key verse, God demands of Job, "Would you even annul my order, treat me as wicked so you can be innocent?"[24]

Yet, if that is all the Voice has to say, the end of the matter is very unsatisfying: "Job, you've got your order of justice, and I have mine. The only difference is that I'm stronger than you are." But there is more. The Voice pursues Job through ironic questioning, asking, in effect,

---

23. Mitchell, *The Book of Job*, p. xviii.
24. E. M. Good, "Job and the Literary Task: A Response," *Soundings* 56 (1973): 479.

WHAT SHALL WE SAY?

Do you really want this moral sense of yours projected onto the universe? . . . Do you want a god who is only a larger version of a righteous judge? . . . If that's the kind of justice you're looking for, you'll have to create it yourself, because that is not *my* justice.[25]

Good question. Do we *really* want our own moral sense projected onto the universe? Well, that depends. What are the other choices? If the only alternative is chaos, I would prefer, frankly, to join my friends and go back to the way things were in Uz. But watch what happens now. The Voice summons forth the two most feared monsters of chaos in the ancient world: Behemoth and Leviathan. These twin ministers of unbridled destruction were the most powerful symbols of ultimate disorder that the ancient Near East possessed. About the best the mythology of that world could hope for was that one day the gods, after pitched battle, would defeat them. But the news about this from God is quite different. "Look at Behemoth," says the Voice. "I created him, and I created you." As for Leviathan, "Can you play with him like a pet sparrow?"

The images here are so incredible that we resist them. We are witnessing the claim that the alternative to our moral scheme of order and disorder is not chaos. It is not even a new and divine scheme of order and disorder. It is, rather, a vision that staggers the imagination, a vision of *only* order, of everything — even that which must be called evil — gathered into the hand of a just God. It is a vision that comes to us from outside the plane of human time, and yet one which serves to give radical hope in the present. As Mitchell expresses it, the Voice is saying, "What is all this foolish chatter about good and evil, . . . about battles between a hero-god and some cosmic opponent? Don't you understand that there is no one else in here?"[26]

By this affirmation, the book of Job anticipates the Christian witness. The New Testament does not claim that suffering is an illusion or that death is a friend. Jesus' own life was marked by suffering with "loud cries and tears," and death is named as a very real and powerful "last enemy." At the same time, the New Testament can affirm that "in Christ all things were created, in heaven and on earth, visible and invisible,

25. Mitchell, *The Book of Job*, p. xxiii.
26. Mitchell, *The Book of Job*, p. xxiv.

whether thrones or dominions or principalities or authorities — all things were created through him and for him. He is before all things, and in him all things hold together" (Col. 1:16-17). The New Testament does not deny the presence of the painful "no" at work in human life. Nor does it attempt to balance this "no" with a countervailing "yes," saying, in effect, that, all things considered, human suffering is not all that terrible. Instead, like Job, it underscores the inescapable reality of that "no," and then offers the death and resurrection of Jesus as the promise that the ambiguous interplay between "no" and "yes" in human experience has ultimately been absorbed into the "Yes" of Christ, who is all in all.

The critics of the book of Job are right, of course. It never does answer Job's aching question, "Why me, Lord?" Instead, Job poses a deeper and finally more searching question: "Do we ultimately want to offer our own scheme of moral order, the very one we employ to determine that some human suffering is unjust, as a replacement for God? Do we want, in other words, to *be* God, or are we willing to move toward being the kind of human being who, even in the midst of inexplicable pain, trusts the One who is God?" It is a Gethsemane-sized decision.

Job's final reply becomes crucial. Many commentators have objected that the NRSV translation of Job 42:6, while possible, is certainly not the only and probably not the best translation of the Hebrew. "I despise myself, and repent in dust and ashes" (meaning "I quit in shame; I want to be neither God nor human") misses the point. Mitchell's rendering surely comes closer to the truth: "I had heard of you with my ears, but now my eyes have seen you. Therefore I will be quiet, comforted that I am dust." Gerald Janzen, whose own translation is similar, maintains that Job's affirmation of himself as "dust" can be seen as

> an act in which the royal vocation of humanity — the royal vocation to *become* humanity — is accepted and embraced with all its vulnerability to innocent suffering. To be dust in God's image is to enjoy and to be responsible for the order manifest in creation; it is to enjoy and be responsible for the freedom which is also manifest in the events of the world and which resides by God's gift in the human soul.[27]

27. Janzen, *Job*, pp. 257-59.

What is striking here is that Job is *not* reduced to nothing. He has become instead what he truly is, a human being, a creature made of dust, living before God in a real world that no longer needs to be sustained by a fantasy. And he takes comfort in that.

The Dawning of a New World

The final scene of the play is not the one we would have expected in the beginning. The language of the old folktale is re-introduced, but the outline of the tale has been stretched to the breaking point, and a new reality emerges in the gap. This is not "paradise regained," but a new creation altogether.

We expected the Adversary to be shamed for his foolish wager, but the Adversary is never mentioned. He has completely disappeared. He is a character suitable only to the old world, which has passed away. The friends of Job are scolded by God for lying, and, according to the old-world theology they so vigorously defended, they should have been punished without mercy. By God's grace, and Job's prayer on their behalf, however, they are in fact forgiven. Job's family and fortunes are not merely restored — they are increased. And an intriguing surprise awaits us here. In the old world, Job's sons are the actors, holding feasts and thoughtfully inviting the sisters along. In the ending, the daughters are on center stage. They are described as the most beautiful women in all the world. They, not the sons, are given names (Dove, Cinnamon, and Eye-Shadow!), and Job performs the unusual act of endowing them, as well as the sons, with a share of his inheritance. Mitchell comments,

> There is something enormously satisfying about this prominence of the feminine at the end of Job. . . . It is as if, once Job has learned to surrender, his world too gives up the male compulsion to control. The daughters almost have the last word. . . . We can't quite figure out why they are so important, but we know that they are.[28]

28. Mitchell, *The Book of Job*, p. xxx.

Finally, there comes the closing of the curtain and the final comments of the narrator. They are an epitaph that expresses all that a person like Job could hope for. Job is one who has learned to trust the God he loves and love the God he trusts. He is a person who has, in the deepest way, learned how to *see* who he is before the true God and find comfort in that. So, "Job lived to see his grandchildren and his great-grandchildren. And Job died, an old man, and full of days."

As we move toward the concluding chapter of this book, this marvelous and complex story of Job comes to us as both warning and promise. It warns us away from the presumption that we will find some solution to the theodicy problem that will somehow "make sense" to us independent of our relationship with God. We do not get to draw a line in the sand and say, "OK, God, when I get this problem of suffering worked out in my mind, I'll step over the line toward you." Or, "OK, God, when you begin to honor my sense of justice, then I will trust you." No, we have to step over the line and fall on our knees in prayer and faith. Only in the light of our trust in God is there anything to see. The promise of the book of Job is that there is indeed much to see in that light, that awe in the presence of God is, indeed, the beginning of wisdom.

CHAPTER FIVE

Walking through the Valley of the Shadow

If you came this way,
Taking any route, starting from anywhere,
At any time or at any season,
It would always be the same: you would have to put off
Sense and notion. You are not here to verify,
Instruct yourself, or inform curiosity
Or carry report. You are here to kneel
Where prayer has been valid.

T. S. Eliot, "Little Gidding," in *Four Quartets*[1]

Why was Christ sent, do you think? Was he sent, as anyone might suppose, to exercise tyranny, to inspire fear and terror? No, in no way. God sent Christ in gentleness and meekness. Yes, God sent Christ as a king might send his son who is a royal son. God sent him as a God. But God also sent him to save human beings, using persuasion, not force, for force is no attribute of God.

Epistle to Diognetus, c. 250[2]

1. T. S. Eliot, "Little Gidding," in *Four Quartets* (New York: Harcourt, 1971), pp. 40-41.
2. Epistle to Diognetus, 2:3-4, author's paraphrase.

The Virtue of Untidiness

Sometimes people assume that preaching works this way: a preacher prepares a sermon during the week, finishes it at some point — maybe Friday afternoon or Saturday night — and then gets up and preaches the finished product in worship on Sunday. This may be the way it appears on the surface, but experienced preachers know better: sermons are never actually finished. There are always loose ends, questions that could have been pursued in more depth, stones left unturned, intriguing aspects of the biblical text unexamined, thoughts not quite fully baked, an untidiness at the heart of things. At some point, though, preachers have to take what they have, stand up, and speak. *Preachers do not preach because the sermon is finished; they preach because it is Sunday. The time has come.*

That sermons are never finished is actually a good thing. Sermons get presented in incomplete form not because of procrastination or negligence — not most of the time, anyway — but because preaching mirrors the character of faithful theology and of the Christian life itself. Karl Barth once described God's revelation as "a bird in flight."[3] By the time we have paused to snap a photo, write a systematic theology, or craft a sermon, the bird has flown on. "All theology is provisional," said theologian Arthur C. McGill. "It is the movement . . . from darkness toward the light, so that as movement no point along its way has permanent or final validity."[4]

This is important wisdom to remember as we attempt, in this concluding chapter, to say as clearly as possible what preachers can and should say about theodicy. If there is one insight we have discovered in our exploration, it is that theodicy is more a pilgrimage toward meaning than it is an answer to a logic problem that we can look up in the back of the book.

So, in our imagination at least, Sunday has now come, and it is time for preachers to stand up and say what we can. We are not going to duck

3. Karl Barth, "The Christian's Place in Society," in *The Word of God and the Word of Man* (Gloucester: Peter Smith, 1978), p. 282.

4. Arthur C. McGill, *Suffering: A Test of Theological Method* (Philadelphia: Westminster Press, 1982), p. 128.

the question. We are going to stay true to our intention to face the question in the form that many thoughtful parishioners frame it, as the impossible chess match, and we are going to try to heed Kushner's warning not to "use big words or clever ways of rephrasing questions in an effort to convince us that our problems are not really problems." But we are going to admit at the outset that what we say here is incomplete, a product of what we can see in the middle of the journey. We see, as Paul said, "through a glass darkly."

Solvitur Ambulando

Solvitur ambulando is a delightful Latin phrase, often associated with Augustine but older in origin, meaning "it is solved by walking." Some speculate that the first time the phrase was used was in a debate between two ancient philosophers, Zeno and Diogenes. Zeno was arguing one of his famous paradoxes — namely, that all motion is really only an illusion. When an arrow's flight is divided into discrete instants in time, in each one of those instants the arrow is only in one place. So, Zeno claimed, if the arrow is always at rest in one instant, it is at rest in all instants. Thus, there is no such thing as motion. Instead of making a counterargument, Diogenes simply got up and walked across the room, saying as he strolled, "Solvitur ambulando."[5]

In regard to other questions, *solvitur ambulando*, "it is solved by walking," means more than the fact that many abstract philosophical problems have practical, down-to-earth solutions. It describes instead a completely different way of knowing, a knowing that comes only to those who are actively engaged in the questions they are asking. In the laboratory, cool detachment is a virtue. If the forensic pathologist is performing an autopsy on a murder victim to determine the cause and time of death, we don't want her to be personally and emotionally invested in the outcome of the investigation, because that could skew the results. We want her instead to be neutral and impartial about the out-

---

5. Clifford Barrett, *Contemporary Idealism in America* (New York: Macmillan, 1932), p. 34.

come and to assess the facts, just the facts. But for some questions, personal and passionate investment in the outcome is not an impediment but an asset, perhaps even a necessity. For instance, suppose you want to know the best way to get to Chattanooga. If you mean the shortest way or the way with the least traffic, then you can be detached and scientific and answer your question by measuring the distance on a map or looking up statistics on traffic volume. But if you mean the most enjoyable way or the most beautiful way or the most interesting way, then you will have to get out on the road yourself and experience the options. *Solvitur ambulando.*

Or, in a deeper sense, suppose I were to say to someone, "You claim that you are my friend, but I am not sure that I trust you. Before I extend my confidence, I would like for you to prove your friendship." Now if my question were one about some scientific fact — say, the boiling point of water — then this person could take me into the lab and prove that water boils at 100 degrees centigrade under standard atmospheric conditions. But *prove* friendship? What could this person say or do? For every reason he extended as to why he was truly my friend, I could say, "Well, he's just saying that to deceive me." To everything he did to prove in advance that he was my friend, I could suspect his motives. Friendship cannot be proved in advance. The only way to know truly that someone is a friend is to walk a distance down life's road with her or him. *Solvitur ambulando.*

The most important theological questions are often "solved by walking" — that is to say, they are questions that yield the deepest insights when they are explored with the eyes of faith. This is the meaning of St. Anselm's famous motto "faith seeking understanding." Anselm did not mean that we are on a journey *from* faith *to* understanding, that we are trying to get beyond faith and move to understanding, as if the goal were to replace blind and naïve faith with more clear-eyed philosophical knowledge. Neither did he mean that "seeking understanding" is a way to prop up faith, looking around for reasons to believe what we already believe. He meant instead that exploring issues and questions as a person of faith can be a bit like looking through night-vision binoculars: faith enables us to see more of what is genuinely there, things we would have missed otherwise. To love God and to walk in faith with

God is to be joyfully drawn into a deeper and deeper understanding of the ways of God.[6]

When Jesus casts out an unclean spirit that had caused a boy to lose his speech and hearing and to experience seizures, an act of healing that his disciples had tried and failed to accomplish, the disciples ask Jesus privately, "Why could we not cast it out?" Jesus responds, "This kind can come out only through prayer" (Mark 9:28-29). In other words, the ministry of casting out evil spirits is not a matter of technique but the manifestation of a life of prayer, a way of walking through life characterized by a constant and faithful relationship to God. Why could we not cast it out? *Solvitur ambulando.*

Several years ago, a ministerial friend of mine went to a summer pastors' conference. At the opening service of worship, my friend was surprised to find himself seated next to his old seminary theology professor from decades back. They had not seen each other for years, and before the service started, they greeted each other warmly and began to catch up. As the service began, the preacher for the evening announced that he was going to preach an "experimental sermon." The experiment was that he would preach for a few minutes and then the congregation would sing a stanza of a hymn. Then the preacher would preach a few more minutes, followed by the next stanza. And so it went, a little preaching, a little hymn-singing, and apparently the experiment was not going well.

My friend leaned over to his old professor and whispered, "My Lord, this is *awful!* In fact, this reminds of something you said in class one day."

The professor looked startled and hissed back, "Something I said in class?"

"Yes," replied my friend, laughing under his breath. "We were studying J. S. Whale's book *Christian Doctrine,* and you said that Whale was a weak theologian because every time he encountered a theological problem he couldn't solve, he quoted a hymn!"

The old professor straightened up in the pew. "Well, I was wrong," he said. "I was young and brash, and I was wrong. Now I realize there are

---

6. Cf. Daniel Migliore, *Faith Seeking Understanding: An Introduction to Christian Theology* (Grand Rapids: Wm. B. Eerdmans, 2004), p. 2.

some theological problems that can be addressed only by singing hymns." *Solvitur ambulando.*

Christians approach deep issues in life, such as the theodicy question, with logic, honest questions, and clear thinking, but they also probe mysteries through praying, singing hymns, participating in worship, and engaging in bold service. In an intriguing essay titled "Working for Liberation: A Change of Perspective in New Testament Scholarship," biblical scholar Luise Schottroff describes how her own involvement with engaged communities of faith and service — her own walking in faith, as it were — changed not only the way she reads the New Testament but the way she understands suffering and hope.[7]

Trained in classical German biblical scholarship, Schottroff learned to observe the protocols of neutral inquiry and to keep her distance intellectually from the raw faith claims of the New Testament. For example, she once shared the consensus view of biblical scholars who employ historical and sociological methods about New Testament eschatology — namely, that the insistence of the New Testament writers that "the Lord is near" and that believers could be filled with hope because God's reign was "close at hand" was seen mainly as a sociological reaction to the disappointment of the early church that Jesus had not yet returned and the promised kingdom of God had not yet arrived. Scholars viewing the New Testament in such a detached fashion could surely understand historically and sociologically how the early church would have developed such views, but these scholars, light-years removed from the social and intellectual situation of the earliest Christians, could never imagine believing such things themselves. Given the fact that twenty centuries have since passed and history rocks along about the same, the New Testament shout that "The Lord is near!" could only be heard as "something like the singing of children in a dark basement."[8]

But then Schottroff, a feminist scholar with strong commitments to liberation movements, began to be involved with Christian groups en-

7. Luise Schottroff, "Working for Liberation: A Change of Perspective in New Testament Scholarship," in *Reading from This Place: Social Location and Biblical Interpretation in Global Perspective,* vol. 2, ed. Fernando F. Segovia and Mary Ann Tolbert (Minneapolis: Fortress Press, 1995), pp. 183-98.

8. Schottroff, "Working for Liberation," p. 198.

gaged on the ground in "liberating practices." These groups did not simply talk about love of enemies and peacemaking as "sublime ideas" — they actively worked for them. They worshiped, prayed, and served every day immersed in the struggle to live and achieve loving, peaceful, and liberating relations. Like their early Christian counterparts, they declared joyfully, "The Lord is near!" and, indeed, they experienced the nearness of God's reign. Now, when Schottroff reads in the New Testament about trumpets on the day of judgment, she does not find herself forced to take that image, and others like it, literally, but neither does she feel inclined to abandon the hope for the nearness of God toward which those images point. "It is my experience," she writes, "that through participation in the struggle for resistance — even if in a very small way — hope does grow."[9] *Solvitur ambulando.*

So what I want to do now is to address the theodicy question by walking . . . walking in the light of Christ. Faith seeking understanding. We will walk down the dark corridors of the questions people have about innocent suffering and the goodness of God, holding as high as we can the lantern of the gospel. We will say what we see as we walk, and we will try to be honest about what we cannot see. We will attempt to reason logically, while admitting that logic and reason can get us only so far. Our prayer as we go will be Anselm's: "I pray, O God, to know thee, to love thee, that I may rejoice in thee."[10]

A Map for the Journey:
The Parable of the Wheat and the Weeds

As we try to pull together what preachers can and should say about theodicy, we will use as a map for our journey one of the parables of Jesus, which, perhaps unexpectedly, represents a profound engagement with and guide for the questions surrounding theodicy. This parable, often called "The Wheat and the Weeds," is found only in Matthew 13:

9. Schottroff, "Working for Liberation," p. 198.

10. Anselm's prayer is found in *St. Anselm: Proslogium; Monologium; An Appendix in Behalf of the Fool by Gaunilon; and Cur Deus Homo?* (LaSalle, Ill.: Open Court Publishing, 1951), p. 178.

He put before them another parable: "The kingdom of heaven may be compared to someone who sowed good seed in his field; but while everybody was asleep, an enemy came and sowed weeds among the wheat, and then went away. So when the plants came up and bore grain, then the weeds appeared as well. And the slaves of the householder came and said to him, 'Master, did you not sow good seed in your field? Where, then, did these weeds come from?' He answered, 'An enemy has done this.' The slaves said to him, 'Then do you want us to go and gather them?' But he replied, 'No; for in gathering the weeds you would uproot the wheat along with them. Let both of them grow together until the harvest; and at harvest time I will tell the reapers, Collect the weeds first and bind them in bundles to be burned, but gather the wheat into my barn.'" (Matt. 13:24-30)

Behind the Scenes

Before we dig into this parable seeking insight about theodicy, we need to do a little background investigation. The Gospel of Matthew has an intricate architecture, a sophisticated design pattern, and if we are going to explore one feature of that design — the Parable of the Wheat and the Weeds — we need to back up and get a look at how this parable fits into the overall structure.

In Matthew 13, seven of Jesus' parables are strung together in one long discourse. This is a literary creation by the author of Matthew. It is not as if Jesus, in his actual ministry, had a day of doing stand-up parables. Matthew has a tendency to group Jesus' teaching into clusters, and here in chapter 13 he has crafted a cluster of parables. The first four parables Jesus delivers from a boat to a great crowd, gathered on the shore of the Sea of Galilee. The other three, Jesus apparently speaks privately only to his disciples.

The first parable in the string is the Parable of the Sower (13:1-9), and after Jesus spoke this parable, the disciples came to him and, in a private conversation, received an explanation of the parable (13:18-23). The fact that Jesus is in a boat on the sea makes this private exchange a bit hard to imagine logistically, but remember, this is a literary construction, and we should not trouble ourselves too much about this practical detail. Matthew's pattern is clear: a public parable followed by a private, in-group explanation aimed at the ears of followers.

The Parable of the Wheat and the Weeds, our focal point, is the second parable in the string, and initially it seems that Matthew is following the very same pattern he employed with "The Sower": the public parable is followed by a private explanation given to his disciples (13:36-43). But here is an odd difference: this time the explanation does not follow the parable immediately. In between the Parable of the Wheat and the Weeds and the explanation, Matthew inserts three additional units of material: two more parables — "The Mustard Seed" (13:31-32) and "The Yeast" (13:33) — and a theological statement by the author about why Jesus speaks in parables (13:34-35). Only after these three texts does Jesus leave the crowd and enter into a house privately with the disciples to explain the parable about the weeds and the wheat. Here is Matthew's account of that exchange:

> Then he left the crowds and went into the house. And his disciples approached him, saying, "Explain to us the parable of the weeds of the field." He answered, "The one who sows the good seed is the Son of Man; the field is the world, and the good seed are the children of the kingdom; the weeds are the children of the evil one, and the enemy who sowed them is the devil; the harvest is the end of the age, and the reapers are angels. Just as the weeds are collected and burned up with fire, so will it be at the end of the age. The Son of Man will send his angels, and they will collect out of his kingdom all causes of sin and all evildoers, and they will throw them into the furnace of fire, where there will be weeping and gnashing of teeth. Then the righteous will shine like the sun in the kingdom of their Father. Let anyone with ears listen!" (Matt. 13:36-43)

This sequence of passages in Matthew raises questions. Why do the disciples ask only about the Parable of the Wheat and the Weeds? Jesus has spoken *three* parables since their last conversation, so why don't the disciples ask Jesus about the other two as well? And since they ask only about the Parable of the Wheat and the Weeds, why is there a separation between the parable and the explanation? As we noted, Matthew 13 is a literary construction. Matthew was free to design any sequence he chose. So why doesn't he do the logical thing and insert the explanation of the Parable of the Wheat and the Weeds immediately after that parable, just like he did after the Parable of the Sower?

The best response to these questions is that Matthew views this whole sequence — (1) the Parable of the Wheat and the Weeds, (2) the Parable of the Mustard Seed, (3) the Parable of the Yeast, (4) the statement about parables, and (5) the private explanation of the Parable of the Wheat and the Weeds — as a cohesive literary swath. He means to arrange the pieces in this order and means for all the pieces to work together. Viewed this way, we can see that the Parable of the Wheat and the Weeds and its explanation serve as the bookends of this literary unit. Jesus starts this unit talking about the wheat and the weeds, and he ends the unit talking about the same thing, which is a strong indication that this parable is the main and controlling event here. This entire unit is about the Parable of the Wheat and the Weeds, and the material in between the bookends — the other two parables and the words about Jesus' parabolic teaching — is designed to complement and clarify the primary parable. I hope we will see how this works as we wind our way through this material.

Trouble in the Fields of God

Now, having explored the background, let us return to the main story, the Parable of the Wheat and the Weeds. Here is what happens: A landowner-farmer sows "good seed" in his wheat field. But during the night, while everyone at the farm is asleep, an enemy comes and sows the seeds of weeds in the field. When these two kinds of seeds sprout and the plants appear, naturally there are weeds and wheat mixed together in the field. Puzzled, the farm laborers go to the owner, asking, "We thought you sowed good seed in the field. Where did these weeds come from?" The owner informs them that an enemy has done mischief, and *that* is why there are weeds in the field. The laborers, eager to set things right, ask the owner if he would like them to pluck the weeds from the field. The owner tells them, no, the attempt to root out the weeds might uproot the wheat as well. The separation of weeds and wheat, he tells them, will be done at harvest time. Then the reapers will be instructed to gather the wheat into the barn and to bind the weeds into bundles to be burned.

Jesus says that the reign of God can be compared to this story. But how? What does the parable mean? Unfortunately, this parable has been mangled by many well-meaning preachers and interpreters, people who take this parable out of context and imagine that Jesus is teaching some abstract and generalized lesson in ethics. Jesus tells the disciples that the field is a metaphor for the world (13:38), so the parable is taken by some flat-footed interpreters to mean that Jesus is teaching that, in this world of good and evil mixed together, we should not presume to try to root out evil. Any attempt to pluck up evil in the world might do more damage than good, so just let it go. Jesus and the angels will take care of it at the end of time.

This interpretation has, of course, monstrous implications. Child abuse? Domestic violence? Economic exploitation? Racism? Millions of gallons of oil spilled into ocean waters and fragile marshlands because of corporate greed and neglect? Let them go. After all, didn't Jesus say that we are not to pluck up the weeds? Not only would this interpretation of the parable, if taken seriously, produce a community of faith that is morally indifferent; it would imply a form of ethical quietism completely at odds with the vision of the rest of the Gospel of Matthew. Already in Matthew we have been told that the "blessed" are merciful peacemakers, people who are the "salt of the earth" and "the light of the world," disciples who hunger so deeply for justice that they get into hot water with the powers and are "persecuted for righteousness' sake." Jesus himself has gone through Galilee healing the sick, casting out demons, and plucking up destructive weeds right and left. If this parable is to find its place in the larger context of Matthew, some other interpretation than "Let evil go" will need to be found.

The parable snaps into proper view when we put it back into its context, both its literary context in Matthew's Gospel and its social and pastoral context in Matthew's community.[11] Matthew's first audience was a young, fragile Christian community thrust into mission in a confusing and morally ambiguous world. They were trying to be and do what Jesus had taught them to be and do, and the results were, frankly, mixed and discouraging. The culture around them was morally conflicted, and the church itself was turning out to be not so pure. Like Christians today who see a world in which warfare is the rule, in which global corporations exploit people and the environment at will, in which suffering seems to fall upon people without rhyme or reason, and who also see a church with clergy who abuse children and treasurers who steal from the offering plate, Matthew's community looked at a hopelessly conflicted world and church and wondered, "What's the use?" Evil and good all mixed together, seemingly intractably. How were they to understand this? How were they to understand the trustworthiness of God in such an environment?

The Parable of the Wheat and the Weeds is addressed to these perplexed Christians, and beyond them to us. It is a piece of congregational wisdom, an exercise in practical theology, a pastoral conversation with

11. Throughout I will be following Matthew's lead and treating the parable as a theological allegory about God, the world, the church, evil, and good. There are, of course, other possibilities for interpreting the parable. Recently, some interpreters have imagined a context for this parable in the ministry of the historical Jesus in which Jesus speaks the story to an audience composed mainly of peasants and tenant farmers. For these hearers, it is argued, the landowner, as a representative of the oppressive ruling class, would not be the "hero" of the tale; in fact, the "enemy," who disrupts Mr. Big's farming plans, would probably be the audience favorite. Taken this way, the parable would be a version of a "trickster tale," in which the underdog ends up getting the best of some authority figure (see, for example, Stanley P. Saunders, *Preaching the Gospel of Matthew: Proclaiming God's Presence* [Louisville: Westminster John Knox Press, 2010]). I find this approach to the parable at best highly speculative and finally unconvincing. Not only does it require that we imagine Matthew to be a saboteur, or at least a bungler, of the oral tradition; it also fails to make any sense of the actual narrative at hand. In its present form, the Parable of the Wheat and the Weeds is neither a trickster tale nor a paradoxical story aimed at stirring up class consciousness. To treat it this way seems more the fruit of an improbable mixture of certain broad assumptions about the socio-economic conditions prevailing in Galilee, a completely hypothetical rewriting of the canonical text, and the ideology of the interpreter. I would find it more convincing to see this parable as entirely the product of Matthew's theological imagination than to think of Matthew wrestling to the ground some provocative piece of social commentary from Jesus and taking it on a forced march in the opposite direction.

anxious believers. When it is understood in this way and in this context, the parable unfolds its deeper meanings, and it also speaks meaningfully to the questions today that equally anxious contemporary Christians have about theodicy.

Where Did These Weeds Come From?

When we recognize the Parable of the Wheat and the Weeds as a pastoral conversation about the presence of evil and good mixed together in the world, we can see that it is an implied dialogue constructed around three urgent questions.

1. God, did you cause this?

Notice that when the servants in Jesus' parable see that the field is weed-infested, they go immediately to the master of the house and demand an accounting. The presence of the weeds is not just an agricultural problem; it raises a question about the character and intention of the one who sowed the fields to begin with. "Master, did you not sow good seed in your field?" Just so and as we have discussed earlier, for people of faith the presence of undeserved suffering in the world is more than a pragmatic and ethical dilemma; it raises questions about the motives of God and the goodness of God. In short, it raises the theodicy question.

A THEODICY OF PROTEST   The first response of theodicy is the cry of the farmworkers in the parable: "We thought you were good and sowed good seed. What is this about?" In other words, "God, did you cause this evil?" An earthquake claims its victims, an infant dies in the crib, a groom is killed in a car accident on the way to his wedding, a woman is raped and murdered in her apartment by an intruder, a sudden burst of turbulence sends an airliner full of crew and passengers plummeting to earth, and we turn as a first impulse in bewilderment and, perhaps, rage to God: "Why, God? Were you in the middle of this, God? Are you to blame for this? God, we thought you sowed good seed!"

Here, then, is a first insight from this parable and one that is by no means insignificant: the gospel enables and empowers the raised fist of protest. Evil and suffering are wounds in creation, and a deeply Christian response is to turn toward God in pain and protest. When we do this, when we confront God in bewilderment or moral outrage over the experience of evil — "How can this be in a good creation? God, how *could* you have allowed this? Could you not have made a better world? Did you cause this evil to be?" — this is not a *lack* of faith but an *expression* of faith. If we did not believe in God at all, or if we believed that God is an absentee landlord or, worse, a cruel tyrant, then the presence of weeds in the wheat, of evil and suffering amid the good, would simply be the way things are. We might despair over the cruelties of life; we might face life stoically; we might curse the day we were born; but it would never occur to us to turn to God and lift up the voice of complaint. Only in expectation that God is good and that the creation is good, only in a relationship of faith and trust, does the presence of evil prompt us to shake the finger of accusation in God's face.

John Claypool was serving as the minister of a Baptist church in Louisville, Kentucky, when his eight-year-old daughter, Laura Lue, a bright and cheerful child who did well in school and relished her violin lessons and ballet classes, was diagnosed with acute leukemia. As a pastor, Claypool had helped many people walk through the valley of the shadow; now he had his own dark valley to face, and he turned to God and demanded an accounting. "When I first heard the diagnosis and went out alone to cry," he said, "I asked the same things anyone would ask: 'Why has this happened? Why do little girls get leukemia? Why is there leukemia at all?'"[12]

The shock of the initial diagnosis was followed by eighteen anguished months of painful treatments, false remissions, and dashed hopes, all leading to that terrible and snowy Saturday afternoon when Claypool watched his daughter take her last breath. In his sermons, Claypool courageously shared his experience of grief with his congregation, and in one sermon he underscored the importance of questioning God:

12. John R. Claypool, *Tracks of a Fellow Struggler: Living and Growing through Grief* (Harrisburg, Pa.: Morehouse Publishing, 2004), pp. 8-9.

Where, then, did we Christians ever get the notion that we must not question God or that we have no right to pour out our souls to God and ask, Why? Did not Job in the Old Testament cry out to God in the midst of his agony and attempt to interrogate the Almighty? Did not Jesus himself agonize with God in Gethsemane, telling God how he felt and what he wanted, and then cry out from the Cross: "My God, My God! Why? Why have you forsaken me?" Would the verse "Ask and it shall be given you, seek and you shall find, knock and it shall be opened unto you" ever have appeared in Holy Scripture if unquestioning acquiescence had been the way to meet tragedy?

. . . There is more honest faith in an act of questioning than in the act of silent submission, for implicit in the very asking is the faith that some light can be given. This is why I found such help in a letter I received from Dr. Carlyle Marney just before Laura Lue died. He admitted that he had no word for the suffering of the innocent and never had, but he said: "I fall back on the notion that God has a lot to give an account for."[13]

That is the first word of the parable: God has a lot to give an account for. Philosopher John Roth is among those Christians who believe that what he calls a "theodicy of protest" is the only adequate response to the question of why there is evil in God's world. If we try to move beyond protest, he argues, if we try to figure out some reason why horrendous evils are a chronic part of human history, we inevitably end up letting God off the hook and thereby demeaning the victims of terrible evil by finding some fancy way to justify their suffering. "Most theodicies," he writes, "have a fatal flaw: they legitimate evil."[14] A "theodicy of protest" gives voice to the silent victims and confronts God: "This is not right, O God! I cannot make room in a good creation for this. I will not try to rationalize it. God, if you are in any way implicated in this, repent!"

Who are we humans to file charges against God? A theodicy of protest, however, is not a cool and reasoned response to the problem of evil;

13. Claypool, *Tracks of a Fellow Struggler,* pp. 56-57.

14. John Roth, "A Theodicy of Protest," in *Encountering Evil: Live Options in Theodicy,* ed. Stephen T. Davis (Louisville: Westminster John Knox Press, 2001), p. 17.

it is the visceral response of people who trust God and feel betrayed. A physician I once met told me, "When I get to heaven — *if* I get to heaven — I'm going to go directly to the throne room of God with a cancer cell in my hand and say, '*Why?*'" Such a bold protest springs from a deep and faithful hunger for God to be loving and just. "A theodicy of protest," Roth says, "both acknowledges and yearns for the love of God."[15]

In his book *A Jew Today,* Nobel laureate and Holocaust survivor Elie Wiesel provides a compelling illustration of how a theodicy of protest rests ultimately on a deep faith. He tells the story of a Jewish family that was driven out of Spain to become wandering nomads, having no land to claim as their own, seeking refuge in vain. One by one, the members of the family died, until only the father remained. In pain over his many losses, he turns his face toward God and cries,

> Master of the Universe, I know what You want — I understand what You are doing. You want despair to overwhelm me. You want me to cease believing in You, to cease praying to You, to cease invoking your name to glorify and sanctify it. Well, I tell You: No, no — a thousand times no! You shall not succeed! In spite of me and in spite of You, I shall shout the Kaddish, which is a song of faith, for You and against You. This song You shall not still, God of Israel.[16]

When we voice protest over the suffering and evil we encounter in life, we do more than just vent our rage. We engage in an ancient and profound form of prayer, an appeal to the honor of God. We must tread carefully here. To imagine in a literal way that God is negligent about or indifferent to suffering until scolded into action by human protest is to think of God far too anthropomorphically. Also, to conceive of prayer as a simple request-response transaction is mechanistic. It is not as if someone in Des Moines were to pray for rain, thus prompting God to reflect, "Well, I had planned for hot and humid today in Des Moines, but now Fred has asked for rain, so rain it is!" Prayer, rather, is a part of our total and ongoing relationship with God, and in ways we do not understand and cannot articulate, God allows our cries, laments, demands, desperate appeals,

15. Roth, "A Theodicy of Protest," p. 16.
16. Elie Wiesel, *A Jew Today* (New York: Random House, 1978), p. 136.

grateful thanksgivings, praises, and protests to be gathered up into God's actions in the world. Understanding prayer as the language of relationship, it makes sense for prayer sometimes to take the form of "God, there is evil in the world. This is not like you! Act to overcome it!"

In some of the psalms, we can hear this kind of prayerful appeal to the honor of God. In Psalm 80, for example, the psalmist points out that the suffering of God's people has made them a laughingstock before other peoples and urges God to overcome the embarrassment:

> Restore us, O God;
>> let your face shine, that we may be saved.
> O LORD God of hosts,
>> how long will you be angry with your people's prayers?
> You have fed them with the bread of tears,
>> and given them tears to drink in full measure.
> You make us the scorn of our neighbors;
>> our enemies laugh among themselves.
> Restore us, O God of hosts;
>> let your face shine, that we may be saved.
>
> (Ps. 80:3-7)

A pastor friend told me about the day a very disturbing telephone call came into the office of the church where he is the pastor. A part-time staff member, who had been out in his neighborhood walking his dog, had been mugged and stabbed in the heart. Rushed to the hospital, he was now in intensive care with virtually no prospect for survival.

When the word spread among the church staff, they gathered spontaneously in the chapel of the church to pray. Standing around the communion table, each person prayed. My friend told me that he and the others offered sincere prayers, but mostly polite and mild petitions, prayers that spoke of comfort and hope and changed hearts, but prayers that had already faced the hard facts of almost certain death.

Then the custodian prayed. My friend reported that it was the most athletic prayer he had ever witnessed. The custodian wrestled with God, shouted at God, anguished with God. His finger jabbed the air, and his body shook. "You've got to save him! You just can't let him die!" he practically screamed at God. "You've done it many times, Lord! You've done it for others. You've done it for me. Now I'm begging you to do it again! Do it for him! Save him, Lord!"

"It was as if he grabbed God by the lapels and refused to turn God loose until God came with healing wings," my friend said. "When we heard that prayer, we just knew that God would indeed come to heal. In the face of that desperate cry for help, God would have been ashamed not to save the man's life." And so it happened.[17]

So, the Parable of the Wheat and the Weeds gives potency and validation to a theodicy of protest. The parable does not stop there, however, and neither can we. Protest alone is not a fully satisfying response to the questions we have about the goodness of God and the presence of innocent suffering. Theodicy is an emotional issue, to be sure, but it is also an intellectual one as well. We want to love God with the heart, but we also want to love God with our mind, too. We want to do more than lament and shout and raise the fist; we also want to understand.

AN ENEMY HAS DONE THIS   When the servants in the parable engage in their own "theodicy of protest," when they confront the landowner with the inescapable evidence of corruption in the fields, demanding to know where the evil weeds have come from, the owner gives a straightforward answer: "An enemy has done this." Just one, simple, declarative sentence — "An enemy has done this" — but, taken theologically, this announcement is breathtaking and complex.

First things first: the landowner is making it clear that he is not the source of the weeds. Seen as a disclosure about the character of the landowner, and thus the moral character of God, it is good news indeed. Sometimes Christians try to "solve" the theodicy problem by trying to figure out why God would cause or allow evil to happen. Maybe God is sending sorrow to shape our character, we say, or perhaps God placed evil in the world to make choosing the good a meaningful moral decision, or maybe we don't understand it now, but eventually we'll know how it is that these sufferings were part of God's good plan all along. To all of these

17. A version of this story appeared in Thomas G. Long, "Living by the Word," *The Christian Century* 123, no. 6 (21 March 2006): 18.

130

justifications of evil, the parable gives a resounding "No!" The cancer that takes a young mother's life, the child brutalized by the predator, the gas ovens at Auschwitz — these are not part of God's "plan"; we will not find out by and by how these events just seemed to be evil but were actually part of the fabric of good. The Sri Lankan father weeping over his dead children, lost in surging seas of the tsunami, will not have to hear us say that one day, in that great beyond, he will understand how this tragedy was really part of God's redemption of the world, as if that could justify his loss, justify God. Did you plant these evil weeds? No, no, a thousand times no! If the first response of a Christian theodicy is protest, the first word of good news is that God did not will this evil, does not cause this evil, and this evil does not come from God, not even from the left hand of God. "God is light and in him there is no darkness at all" (1 John 1:5).

Years ago, a student graduated from the seminary where I was then teaching, and became the pastor of her first congregation. She made it her goal, since her church was small, to visit the entire membership roll during the first six months that she was there. At the end of six months, she had almost done it. She had visited everybody but one family. This family had not attended church in a couple of years, and the new pastor was advised by one of the officers, "Leave them alone. They aren't coming back."

But she'd set a goal for herself, and one afternoon she drove to the family's home and knocked on the door. Only the wife was at home, and, when the pastor introduced herself, the woman invited her in for a cup of coffee. They sat at the kitchen table and chatted. They chatted about this, they chatted about that, and then they talked about *it*. Two years before, the wife had been vacuuming in the back bedroom while her infant son played in the den. She hadn't checked on him in a while, so she snapped off the vacuum cleaner and went into the den. He wasn't there. She traced her son's probable path across the den, through the open patio door, across the patio to the swimming pool, where she found him.

"Our friends at church were very kind," she said. "They told us it was God's will." The young minister put her coffee cup down on the table. Should she touch that or not? She decided to touch it.

"Your friends at church meant well, but they were wrong. It wasn't God's will. God doesn't will the death of children."

Surprisingly, the mother's jaw clenched, her face reddened, and she said in anger, "Well then, *who* do you blame? Are you blaming *me*? Are you blaming *me* for this? Is that what you're saying?"

"No, no — I'm not blaming you," the pastor responded, now on the defensive. "I'm not blaming you, but I'm not blaming God, either. God was as grief-stricken by your son's death as you are." But the woman's face remained frozen in rage, and it was clear that this conversation was over.

Returning to the church, the young minister kicked herself. "I shouldn't have touched it," she said to herself. "I should have left well enough alone." But when she got back to her office, there was a message waiting from the wife on her answering machine. "I don't know where this is going," the trembling recorded voice said, "but my husband and I want you to come out and talk to us about this. For two years we've thought God was angry at us, but now we wonder if it's not the other way around."

Despite the obvious risk, this young pastor was right to affirm that it was not God's will that this child die. It is not the gospel either to pretend that evil is not evil but only good in disguise, or to see the hand of God causing evil, even for ulterior purposes.

Some could object, pointing out that often good does come out of evil. The collapse of a building in an earthquake results in new building codes that save many lives in the future. A death in a family brings new closeness to the survivors. It could also be argued that sometimes what we call "evil" turns out to be good, a blessing in disguise. But even though we may be able to point to examples of good coming out of evil, we must nevertheless resist the temptation to resolve the theodicy question by saying that, when all is said and done, we'll understand the reasons why there was evil in creation and how, in the final analysis, what we called "evil" served God's good purposes. This "solution" to the impossible chess match essentially attempts to redefine the claim "There is innocent suffering" by saying, "Well, yes, innocent people suffer, but taken in cosmic perspective, this suffering ended up for the good."

There are two principal reasons why we must resist this response to theodicy. The first is that the examples of evil that turned out to be blessings in disguise — say, the heart attack that shocked someone into a life of better health and deeper purpose — are not really the best test cases. As Marilyn McCord Adams has reminded us, it is the cases of catastrophic evil, of horrendous evil, of evil that is malicious, random, meaningless, and absurd, evil that has no possible redemptive purpose, that must finally be accounted for.[18] It is not sufficient to have a Christian theodicy that "works" only for those experiences of evil that turn out to have a silver lining.

The second reason is found, as we have seen in Chapter 4, in Ivan's profoundly Christian response to evil in *The Brothers Karamazov*. Ivan describes a military officer cruelly and meaninglessly torturing a little girl to death in front of her mother. He can imagine a future kingdom in which all has been forgiven and everyone has been reconciled. Both the child and the mother have forgiven the torturer. Ivan recognizes that what has been lost is the morality of God. If God's heaven requires the torture of one child, Ivan says, then he respectfully declines the ticket of admission.

The unequivocal "no" of the parable, then, is gospel indeed. God does not plant evil in the fields of our lives and creation. God does not create evil so that we will have free moral choice, so that we will have our souls formed, so that we will have our sins punished, as a part of some "best possible world" scenario, or for any other purpose.

Well, then, where did the weeds come from? "An enemy has done this" is the landowner's reply. Although, as we shall see, this response raises some tough questions, it should first be heard as the powerful good news that it is. Evil is God's enemy. Not God's instrument, not God's counterpart, not something about which God is indifferent. Evil is God's *enemy*, period. To the father standing empty-armed and broken-hearted in the surf of the Indian Ocean, to the grief-stricken woman at the grave of her young husband, to the parents of the stillborn child, to the despairing residents of a devastated Haitian city, an important word of the gospel is that this evil which has risen up to destroy life and to break the human spirit is God's enemy, too.

But to say that the evil present in creation comes from God's "en-

18. Marilyn McCord Adams, *Horrendous Evils and the Goodness of God* (Ithaca, N.Y.: Cornell University Press, 1999), p. 26.

emy" immediately raises some thorny questions. Who is this enemy? Where did this enemy come from? How did an enemy get into God's good creation?

When we look at Jesus' explanation of the parable, we find that the enemy is "the devil." For Matthew, this identification was evidently sufficient. God is at work in the world, but so is the devil, and *that* is why there are weeds in the wheat. Not many contemporary Christians, however, will be able to leave it at this. Matthew may speak of "the devil," and Martin Luther may have been able to sing "And though this world, with devils filled, should threaten to undo us," what sense can talk of the devil make to thoughtful people today?

Plenty, as a matter of fact. "The devil" is best imagined not literally, as some demonic figure lurking in the shadows, but as a symbol of a deep theological truth — namely, that the evil we experience in history is more than the sum of its parts and transcends logical explanation. The horror of the Holocaust, the genocide in Rwanda, the massacre at My Lai, the cruelties of those who prey upon and kill children for sexual gratification — none of these forms of evil, or others, can be fully accounted for by political, anthropological, or psychological explanations. There is a dark spiritual force in evil as we experience it.

Think, for example, of any parent who has struggled with a son or daughter hopelessly caught in the downward and suicidal spiral of serious addiction to narcotics. Yes, we can analyze the chemical aspects of addiction, the psychological brokenness, the existential despair, the negative social influence of peers, but none of these explanations, even in combination, can fully encompass the will to self-destruction, even at times the perverse delight in it, the rage toward self and others, the hopelessness and inability to will what the mind knows is the good. The parent realizes that the child is captive to forces beyond rational control, knows that the child is up against more than mere human failings, recognizes in the heart the truth of the biblical claim "For our struggle is not against enemies of blood and flesh, but against the rulers, against the authorities, against the cosmic powers of this present darkness, against the spiritual forces of evil in the heavenly places" (Eph. 6:12).

To say that the enemy is the devil is not to revert to pre-scientific fairytale images but to say, through the ancient language of Scripture, that evil has a cosmic, trans-human reality. Evil is not just a failing; it is a force. The American soldiers who murdered the elderly and children in the massacre at My Lai in the Vietnam War were, for the most part, ordinary young men with good morals and no desire to do evil. But something, as we say, "just came over them." Evil is not merely a problem; it is a mystery. Problems can be solved — more accurate earthquake prediction, a drug to cure cancer, better training for soldiers, a political program to eliminate poverty — but evil is pernicious and resists solutions. Its persistence even in the face of our best efforts to mature as a human race and to build a just society is a deep mystery, a mystery that can be experienced and explored but not solved. The Scripture teaches this, but we know this is so also because human experience in all generations has demonstrated its truth.

Whatever it is "out there" in creation, and also "in here" in the human heart — the powers of death, the random and absurd force of evil, "the pestilence that stalks in darkness . . . the destruction that wastes at noonday" (Ps. 91:6) — it is not only our enemy; it is God's enemy, too.

But where does it come from, this enemy of life and of God? Here we must, in humility, admit that our light shines only partway into the darkness. We cannot see everything, and Christians must remain to some degree agnostic about the origins of evil, willing to admit what cannot be known. But we can see some things, and we should say what we do see. Four main logical possibilities present themselves for how it was that evil got mixed into a good creation:

1. God is the author of both good and evil and made the creation as a mixture of good and evil, for whatever divine reasons.
2. There are two "creators," a good one and a bad one. God is the author of the good aspects of creation, and the force of evil is the author of the bad ones.
3. God did not fashion the creation *ex nihilo* — that is, out of nothing — but started with some raw materials already at hand. As for the origins of these raw materials, we cannot say, but the potential for evil was already present in them, like impurities in clay. God's creation is a work in progress, and all of the evil has not yet been eliminated.
4. God is the one and only creator, and the creation was made "very

good." But something happened after God's creative act to introduce evil into the goodness of creation.

When we understand the question we are asking to be not an issue of abstract metaphysics but a pastoral and practical theological question, and when we shine the light of Christ, the light of the gospel, on the question, I am convinced that only option 4 remains as a live option. Option 1 makes God the author of evil, the sower of the weeds as well as the wheat, and this, as we have already discussed, is not the God we meet in Christ. Option 2, popular among the early Christian Gnostics, is irretrievably dualistic and forces us to imagine creation as the eternal battleground of two rival deities. Option 3, taken up by some process theologians, requires the positing of a reality antecedent to the reality of God and all but demands the construction of a mythic narrative in which Yahweh, the God of Jesus, arrives on stage late in the game and begins to influence an already existing creation.

What we see in the light of the gospel is that God is altogether good, and everything that exists comes from the hand of God. "All things came into being through him, and without him not one thing came into being" (John 1:3). God is not the author of evil, and "every perfect gift is from above, coming down from the Father of lights, with whom there is no variation or shadow" (James 1:17).

So, what happened? How did the enemy with a bagful of malicious seed get into the good creation? Here our light shines only so far into the shadows. In our faithful memory are ancient mythic stories that are like potent dreams only half-remembered at the break of day, memories of a wild and powerful creation, formed by God but with its own fierceness, a creation in which the sea "bursts out from the womb" (Job 38:8) and "the wild animals play" in freedom (Job 40:20); memories of a cosmic rebellion in which good creatures somehow turned against God; memories of a wounded creation groaning "in labor pains" and waiting in hope for redemption (Rom. 8:22-23).

As a satisfying explanation for what happened, as we have already seen in previous chapters, none of these memories altogether works. These stories do not explain how evil got into the world; rather, they affirm some truths about it — namely, that it did not come from the hand of God, that it is an intruder into the goodness of creation, that human beings have become entangled and complicit in it, that the creation has become anguished and in pain, groaning under the burden of evil and suffering, and that this evil is God's enemy. Any event of evil is full of complexities and resists easy analysis. We do not know all that we would like to know. We are in the middle of things, and we cannot see all the way to ultimate causes.

This means that Christian faith affirms what David Bentley Hart has called "a kind of 'provisional' cosmic dualism."[19] It is dualism because it recognizes that there is evil in the world and that this evil is not of divine origin but is God's enemy. It is cosmic because it recognizes that evil is a spiritual force; it is not just a result of human error, natural forces, and understandable conflict, but is rather a force that transcends human capacities and rational explanation. It is provisional because it rejects the idea that this battle between good and evil was an original feature of creation or an enduring one. Evil was not present on the seventh day of creation, when God rested, and it will not be present at the end of time, when all creation will enter its Sabbath rest. But here in the middle of time, evil, God's enemy, is a constant presence and a fact of life.

2. Can we fix it?

The second question the servants in the parable ask is "Do you want us to gather the weeds?" If the landowner did not sow the weeds and does not want the weeds, then perhaps the thing to do is to root them out. The landowner's answer is "No, for in gathering the weeds you would uproot the wheat along with them" (Matt. 13:29). This "no" from the landowner is, from the outset, an assault on human arrogance. To assume that we could go out into the field and pluck up all of the weeds of evil drastically underestimates the character of evil and drastically overestimates our own power for good.

A decade ago, right after the attacks of September 11, 2001, a daily newspaper carried this unintentionally satirical headline: "[President] Bush Vows to Rid the World of Evildoers." Bush's claim was a piece of po-

---

19. David Bentley Hart, *The Doors of the Sea* (Grand Rapids: Wm. B. Eerdmans, 2005), p. 62.

litical rhetoric, of course, but to take it with any seriousness at all would mean that the president would have had to purge the world of all terrorists and murderers, but then he would have needed to keep on eliminating people — burglars, embezzlers, drug dealers, and Wall Street con artists, to name a few — finally ridding the world of himself and all of the rest of us, too, since all of us are, in some measure, "evildoers." Evil and good are deeply entwined, in history and in ourselves. We do not have the wisdom or the power to take tweezers and pry them apart, to pluck up the weeds from the wheat field.

In the 1950s, when I was a child, one of my Sunday school friends was a girl stricken with polio. Her legs were twisted and paralyzed, and she was confined for a while to an iron lung, which assisted her labored breathing. The fact that my own children, when they were young, never had to see a friend in an iron lung, I count as one of the gracious gifts of God. Right at the moment that my friend was suffering with the ravages of that terrible disease, Jonas Salk, in a lab in Pittsburgh, was perfecting a vaccine that prevented polio. But it was not available until 1955, too late for my friend.

She is in her sixties now, her body still twisted by the virus that attacked her in her childhood. She makes her way awkwardly on crutches. I have walked on my legs every day of my life; she has not walked on hers since she was six years old. But the moment she enters a room, the level of grace is elevated greatly. She lights up with joy every place she touches. She is a college professor and an artist, an accomplished human being with profound gifts. I have been strong all my life where she has been weak, yet she has qualities of character and joy and faith and hope that I can only aspire to.

Now, what do I think about the evil she has endured? Do I think God gave her polio? No, a thousand times no! "Did you cause this; did you sow these weeds?" No! Do I think God placed polio in her life for the purpose of soul-making? No, a thousand times no! Do I think her soul has been formed by this? Yes. If someone handed me a magic wand now and gave me the power to change anything about her past, to pluck up the weeds from the wheat, I think I would want to wave it and banish the polio, make it so she never suffered from that disease. But to tell you the truth, I really wouldn't know where the limits of my wisdom were. She is a beautiful and radiant human being, and I wouldn't know what to take away from the personal history that brought her to this place. In short, I might want to "fix it," but I lack the discernment to do so.

There is, however, another implication of the landowner's "no," one that is theologically more subtle. The servants are forbidden to run roughshod into the field, plucking up the weeds, not only because they lack the wisdom to do so without damaging the wheat, but also because *this is not God's way in the world*. The impulse of the servants to rush out into the fields and to begin ripping out the evil weeds rests finally on their assumption that this is what the landowner would want, that this is the way the landowner would dispatch the problem of evil. The world is a mixed field, good and evil all mixed up and out there in plain view, but it is not the way of God to charge into the field with a scythe, chopping away at the weeds.

This brings us face-to-face with the urgent question that has reverberated through the centuries of the theodicy problem: *Why* is this not God's way with evil? If genetic disorders, like that suffered by Harold Kushner's son, take the lives of innocent children, if tsunamis rise up to devastate villages, if a twisted psyche sends a madman to the top of a tower to shoot random people below, then why doesn't God stop this evil? As Bart Ehrman screamed inwardly at that Christmas Eve worship service, "Why *doesn't* [God] enter into the darkness again? Where is the presence of God in this world of pain and misery? Why is the darkness so overwhelming?"[20] We want God to use divine power, to rend the heavens and come down to put a halt to the ravages of evil.

Language is crucial here, and we must be careful about how we speak. There are at least two ways of answering the question "Why doesn't God stop evil?" that are near misses. First, we recall that Rabbi Kushner and some others say that God does not forcefully root out evil because God *cannot* do so; God *lacks the power* to do so. The idea that God lacks the power to thwart evil is a miss, but, ironically, it is a near miss. In the New Testament, Jesus performs many "deeds of power," but his power is often displayed in ways that do not conform to classical views of divine omnipotence. Jesus has power, but so do the demonic forces, and sometimes the

---

20. Bart D. Ehrman, *God's Problem: How the Bible Fails to Answer Our Most Important Question — Why We Suffer?* (New York: HarperOne, 2008), p. 5.

balance between the two seems tenuous. We even have in the Gospel of Mark a story about the failure of Jesus' power. When the hometown folk in Nazareth resist Jesus, Mark says that Jesus *"could do no deed of power there, except that he laid his hands on a few sick people and cured them"* (Mark 6:5, italics added).

But here is a paradox: the Gospel writers, even when they present Jesus' divine power as nuanced or limited in practice or in agonized and sometimes uncertain combat with the power of evil, never do so because they understand God's power somehow to be restricted or insufficient. To the contrary, the New Testament rests on the conviction that God is indeed all-powerful. For example, when Jesus was arrested in Gethsemane, one of his followers attempted to protect Jesus by drawing a sword. This flourish of swordplay was not Jesus' kind of power, and Jesus stopped him, saying, "Put your sword back into its place; for all who take the sword will perish by the sword" (Matt. 26:52). But then Jesus added, "Do you think that I cannot appeal to my Father, and he will at once send me more than twelve legions of angels? But how then would the scriptures be fulfilled, which say it must happen in this way?" (Matt. 26:53-54). The implication is clear enough: the omnipotent God *could* have sent in the angelic troops to halt the evil at hand, but this kind of power play is not the way of God.

This leads to the second theological near miss in response to the question "Why doesn't God stop evil?" It is tempting to say, "God *could* wipe out evil if God wanted to do so, but God *chooses,* for God's own reasons, not to do so." There is, again, a measure of truth here. God, hypothetically, could have sent those angelic troops to save Jesus, but Jesus did not call for them, and God did not send them. So, in a way it is true: God could, but God didn't. The problem with this way of phrasing the issue is that it depicts God as detached from the world and divine action regarding evil as a set of equally viable options, almost as if God is in some distant heaven sitting in front of a control panel with buttons labeled "(A) Stop evil," "(B) Don't stop evil, but make things somewhat better," "(C) Don't stop evil, but inspire people to act bravely," "(D) Do nothing," and so on, trying to choose which button to push. This carries obvious negative implications about God's character. If a predator is about to murder a child and God, mulling over choices, could halt this act but does not push the "Stop evil" button, then it is hard to avoid the conclusion that God is morally malfeasant.

So if these two ways of phrasing the matter — "God lacks the power to stop evil" and "God could stop evil, but chooses not to" — are misses, however near they may be, then is there a more faithful response to the question "Why doesn't God stop evil?" Yes, I believe there is, but it may be hard to accept, at least at first. Why doesn't God come into the fields of life and root out all suffering and evil? Because God *cannot* do so in the way we want God to do so. However, "cannot," as used here, means something altogether different from the claims about divine power made by Kushner. God cannot root out evil, but not because God lacks the power. God cannot root out evil because engaging the world in this way would require a different god. A god who used power in this way, in the way we often imagine God should do it, would not be true to God's own character, would not be the God we know in Jesus Christ.

What exactly does this mean? Whenever we imagine how God, to our way of thinking, should respond to evil, we inevitably project ourselves large. In other words, we think how *we* would respond to evil, if we had God's great power. If, say, we visit a pediatric oncology ward and see children suffering and dying from cancer, we are moved by their distress and cannot understand how God could allow this suffering. If *we* were God, we say to ourselves, we would immediately put a stop to this. But we know we are not God, so we cry out in our hearts, "O that you would rend the heavens and come down. O that you would put a stop to this suffering!" In this way, we are pleading for the warrior God to come and destroy this evil at once. We are praying for God to act like we would act if we were God, to display, in other words, power, as human beings define power, in full array, and to destroy without delay what is so clearly an evil. We would do this; so, why doesn't God do it?

But do we really know what we are praying for? Suppose God *were* to come in the way that we desire, and not just to the cancer ward (why stop there?), but to all of life to wipe off the face of the earth every speck of evil? Suppose God were to come as we imagine, come as a warrior with a sword, cutting out every vestige of evil — all disease, all greed, all violence, all hatred, all sloth — come as a ruthless farmer with a machete, slashing away at every weed? Who could stand? Every one of us is entangled in evil. None of our relationships is pure — spouse-spouse, parent-child, friend-friend, colleague-colleague, clan-clan, nation-nation — and if God would come with a vengeance to root out evil, what is there human that could survive? One is reminded of the famous saying of a military officer about a battle in the Vietnam War: "It became necessary to destroy the town to save it."

So, we should count it grace that God does not answer our prayer as we imagine. But that does not mean that God does not answer our prayer. When we cry out, with and on behalf of all suffering humanity, "O God, that you would rend the heavens and come down," God does indeed answer. What if God answers our prayer, only not as we imagine? What if God does "rend the heavens and come down" to do battle against the enemy of cancer and all other forms of evil, but not on our terms, but in a way true to the character of God? What if God does come as a warrior, but not as a warrior who fights like a human combatant, but as a warrior God who fights only with the weapons of love? God is indeed all-powerful, but God's power is not like raw human power but is instead a love that takes the form of weakness, a power expressed most dramatically on the cross. We think we want God to plunge into creation with a machete and to slash away at evil. It is not that this is somehow out of God's range of power; it is that this kind of use of power is out of God's range of character.

By analogy, imagine that auditors have uncovered missing funds in a certain company's books, and the bookkeeper falls under immediate suspicion of embezzlement. When the bookkeeper's wife learns that her husband has been accused of being a thief, she replies in astonishment, "It isn't true! My Ralph could *never* steal anything." Now what does she mean that Ralph could never steal anything? Does she mean that Ralph technically lacks the power to pilfer funds? No, Ralph has that potential and could have used it. What she means is that she knows her husband and that stealing isn't in his moral makeup. If he had stolen the money, he wouldn't be the husband she knows and loves; he wouldn't be *Ralph*.

Just so, if God exercised some hypothetical power option and were to blow through the walls of creation wielding a sword of conventional power and bringing down the hand of divine wrath against evil, then God wouldn't be the God we know in Christ. God wouldn't be *God*. Japa-

142

nese theologian Kosuke Koyama describes the contrast between human conceptions of power and the way power should be understood in the light of Christ:

> The name, Jesus Christ, is not a magic name which transforms the broken world into an instant paradise. . . . The name of Jesus Christ is not a powerful name in the manner of the imperial power. It is a "foolish and weak" name (1 Cor. 1:21-25)! . . . Jesus Christ is not a quick answer. If Jesus Christ is the answer, he is the answer portrayed in the crucifixion![21]

The theologian Jürgen Moltmann observes that, when it comes to evil and suffering, we want God to perform a dramatic miracle, like Jesus did, healing the man with the withered arm, raising up a little girl from her deathbed. But the miracles of Jesus did not themselves eliminate evil and death. They were signs of a deeper healing, but they did not in themselves accomplish this healing. All of the people Jesus healed and raised from death are now dead; on the plane of human history, the power of death has claimed them all. As Moltmann says,

> *Healing* vanquishes illness and creates health. Yet it does not vanquish the power of death. But *salvation* in its full and completed form is the annihilation of the power of death and the raising of men and women to eternal life. In this wider sense of salvation . . . people are healed not through Jesus' miracles, but through Jesus' wounds; that is, they are gathered into the indestructible love of God.[22]

People are healed not through miracles, but through the wounds of Jesus. God is at work in the world battling the enemy, not with the power of the sword but with the "weak" power of the crucifixion. So, the landowner in the parable tells the servants not to try to pluck up the weeds, not merely because they do not have the discernment to do this, but

---

21. Kosuke Koyama, *Mount Fuji and Mount Sinai: A Pilgrimage in Theology* (London: SCM Press, 1984), p. 241.

22. Jürgen Moltmann, *The Way of Jesus Christ* (Minneapolis: Fortress Press, 1993), pp. 108-10.

WHAT SHALL WE SAY?

mainly because ripping out evil is not the way of God in the world. That leaves the servants — and us — with one more set of questions: If it is not God's way to pluck up evil, then what becomes of it? What is God doing about it? And what becomes of our faith in the goodness of God?

3. Will it always be this way?

Although it is not explicitly stated in the text, there is an implied question between the prohibition — "No, do not attempt to gather the weeds" — and what follows next in the parable. If we don't pluck up the weeds, the servants wonder, what happens to them? Do they just grow wild and out of control? Will the weeds of evil always be there?

The parable ends with a promise: No, the weeds will not always be there. At harvest time, the reapers will collect the weeds first to be burned, and the wheat will be gathered into the barn. In the explanation of the parable, this image is given an eschatological frame: the harvest is the end of the age, and "the Son of Man will send his angels, and they will collect out of his kingdom all causes of sin and all evildoers, and they will throw them into the furnace of fire" (Matt. 13:41-42). The righteous, on the other hand, "will shine like the sun" (Matt. 13:43).

This ending to the parable contains an eschatological vision that the loving power of God will finally destroy all evil. It is a function of Matthew's rhetoric to personalize evil (evil = "evildoers"), but the import is wider and deeper. The overall vision is sublime: The ravenous beast of evil, which has soaked history in blood and tears, will be completely eradicated. Every tear will be dried, and death and pain will be no more.

In the little village of Dachau, Germany, there is a museum of the Holocaust on the forbidding grounds of the old Nazi concentration camp. In the museum, there is a photograph so haunting that everyone who sees it, secular or religious, utters a kind of prayer. The photograph is of a mother and her little girl being marched to the gas chamber at Auschwitz. There is not one thing that the mother can do to stop what is happening, so she commits the only act of love she has left. She walks behind her daughter and places her hand over her daughter's eyes, so she will not have to see where she is going. Everyone who encounters this terrible photo cries out some version of "O God, do not let that be the last word. Do not let whatever that beast is, in us and history, have the power to tell the final story of this little girl, of these people, or of any of us." I am promising you, said Jesus in this parable, that this evil does not get the last word. Standing at the end of time is the just judge whose righteousness shines like the sun, the risen Christ. Whatever beast mauls its way through history, sending little girls to a cruel death, will be utterly destroyed.

Here is the paradox: The love of God, seemingly so weak on the cross, ends up victorious and ultimately destroys the power of evil. Here, it seems to me, a comprehensive theodicy from a Christian perspective parts company with more timid approaches. The nonviolence of God's love ultimately does violence to evil. The Prince of Peace is, in regard to cosmic evil, the divine warrior.

If a little boy is attacked by bullies and beaten up every day after school, he wants more than sympathy from his parents. He wants justice. He wants his suffering to count to someone, and he wants the beatings stopped and the perpetrators judged. Indeed, if someone doesn't take up his cause, he will have no other recourse than to plot revenge on his own. Just so, theologian Miroslav Volf has argued that the gospel appeals to live with forgiveness and nonviolence rest firmly on the confidence that God will finally destroy evil and establish justice. The only way human beings can put down the sword and turn the other cheek is when they know that God has declared war on evil. As Paul said, "Beloved, never avenge yourselves, but leave room for the wrath of God; for it is written, 'Vengeance is mine, I will repay, says the Lord.'" Volf writes:

> My thesis that the practice of nonviolence requires belief in divine vengeance will be unpopular with many Christians, especially theologians in the West. To the person who is inclined to dismiss it, I suggest imagining that you are delivering a lecture in a war zone. . . . Among your listeners are people whose cities and villages have been first plundered, then burned and leveled to the ground, whose daughters and sisters have been raped, whose fathers and brothers have had their throats slit. The topic of the lecture: a Christian attitude toward violence. The thesis: we should not retaliate because God is perfect noncoercive love. Soon you

would discover that it takes the quiet of a suburban home for the birth of the thesis that human nonviolence corresponds to God's refusal to judge. In a scorched land, soaked in the blood of the innocent, it will invariably die.[23]

I would modify Volf's statement in only one way: it is, I think, a central paradox of the Christian faith that God is indeed perfect noncoercive love, but that this perfect love, poured out on the cross, burns down the gates of hell and destroys the powers of evil and death. How this happens, we do not know, but for those who stand open-mouthed in astonishment at Easter's empty tomb, we know it is true. And it is the risen Christ, the wounds still marking his hands, who will send angels, and they, in the words of the parable, "will collect out of his kingdom all causes of sin and all evildoers, and they will throw them into the furnace of fire."

But no matter how beautiful and encouraging may be this vision of evil vanquished, of peace and righteousness at the end of time, it is not enough. Process theology fails, in part, because it has no real eschatology. The process simply goes on *ad infinitum;* there never comes a time when "the strife is o'er, the battle is done," when righteousness shines like the sun, and the Easter victory of God is complete. But purely future-oriented visions of God's victory also fail. Yes, God will one day stand victorious, evil conquered, but there is too much tragedy and suffering on the road to get there. There may come a day when evil is thrown into the fire and the angels will dance and sing in the bright light of God's conquest, but if it leaves in its wake the countless dead of tsunamis and earthquakes, the terrified cries of the little girl on the way to the gas chamber, then, as Dostoevsky's Ivan said, "they have put too high a price on harmony."

If there is to be a genuinely Christian response to theodicy, it must bear witness to the ultimate victory of God, to that time when God "will wipe every tear from their eyes. Death will be no more; mourning and crying and pain will be no more, for the first things have passed away" (Rev. 21:4). But it must also bear witness to what God is doing now, in the

---

23. Miroslav Volf, *Exclusion and Embrace: A Theological Exploration of Identity, Otherness, and Reconciliation* (Nashville: Abingdon Press, 1996), p. 304.

midst of history, in the midst of pain and suffering, to address evil. In his book *Becoming Human,* Jean Vanier, the founder of the L'Arche communities, describes a troubling visit he made to the children's ward of a mental health hospital:

> I once visited a psychiatric hospital that was a kind of warehouse of human misery. Hundreds of children with severe disabilities were lying, neglected, on their cots. There was a deadly silence. Not one of them was crying. When they realize that nobody cares, that nobody will answer them, children no longer cry. It takes too much energy. We cry out only when there is hope that someone may hear us.[24]

We cry out only when there is hope that someone may hear us. It would do little to comfort these children who lie in hopeless silence to assure them that one day the evil that now robs them of dignity and fullness of life will lie in ruins. What about now? Does God hear them now? Does God come to them in their distress?

The response of the gospel is yes. Yes, God hears the cries of the suffering. Yes, God comes with healing in God's wings. God comes, in fact, as a warrior. The suffering and pain of these children are the enemies of God. From our perspective in the middle of history, we do not know everything about where this evil came from, but we know that it is God's mortal enemy, and God comes to do combat, comes in the power of the cross, comes in the power of love.

The active work of God taking on the enemy of evil in the middle of tragic history is the message of the two parables inserted between the Parable of the Wheat and the Weeds and its explanation. First there is the Parable of the Mustard Seed:

> He put before them another parable: "The kingdom of heaven is like a mustard seed that someone took and sowed in his field; it is the smallest of all the seeds, but when it has grown it is the greatest of shrubs and becomes a tree, so that the birds of the air come and make nests in its branches." (Matt. 13:31-32)

24. Jean Vanier, *Becoming Human* (Toronto: House of Anansi Press, 1998), p. 9.

What does this parable have to do with the Parable of the Wheat and the Weeds? To begin with, this parable presents as an image of the kingdom of God, the reign of God, a mustard bush, a plant that is simultaneously both valuable and suspiciously like a weed. Writing in the first century, about the same time as Matthew, Pliny the Elder said of the mustard plant that "with its pungent taste and fiery effect, it is extremely beneficial for health," but on the other hand, it runs amok in the garden, and "once been sown, it is scarcely possible to get the place free from it."[25] No wonder the servants in the main parable are commanded not to try to pull up the weeds; it is hard to tell whether the kingdom itself is weed or not! Also, God's power at work in the world does not look very potent, large, or worthy. It is like a tiny seed that grows into an enormous and embracing mustard shrub that provides shelter for the birds of the air. In other words, God is at work in the world, but it doesn't look like it. From all appearances, God's action in the world is too small, too insignificant to count. But it turns out to be powerfully effective, becoming "the greatest of shrubs" (Matt. 13:32).

Then comes the Parable of the Yeast:

> He told them another parable: "The kingdom of heaven is like yeast that a woman took and mixed in with three measures of flour until all of it was leavened." (Matt. 13:33)

Everything about this parable is counterintuitive. God's kingdom, God's reign, God's power in the world is compared to yeast. We think of yeast as a good thing, something that makes bread rise, but not so in the ancient world. In the Bible, yeast is never a good thing; it is a corrupting agent. Not only that, but this yeast is taken by a woman, a gender not associated with power, and what does the woman do? She "mixes" the yeast into a huge amount of flour. But the Greek is stronger: she doesn't just mix the yeast, she "encrypts" it; she smuggles the yeast into the flour, and the yeast pervades and affects everything. In short, the kingdom is a stealth operation. A person with no conventional power takes a corrupting agent and smuggles it into the flour, changing everything. God's

25. Pliny the Elder, *Natural History,* Volume V, Libra XVII-XIX (Cambridge: Harvard University Press, 1938), p. 529.

power, the parable states, is like this. It does not look like power, but it is out there undercover, encrypted, hidden from view, but nonetheless bringing everything under its sway.

Putting all this together, what can we say? God's power in the world is ambiguous. It doesn't look like power — in fact, it looks suspiciously like a worthless weed that we'd like to root out of the field — but it is nevertheless working, in stealth fashion, to produce something of great size and pervasive impact. And the reason Jesus presents all this in parables, in riddles, is that he is disclosing what has always been true, but has been "hidden from the foundation of the world" (Matt. 13:35).

O Lord, We Cry unto You

Where have we come in regard to theodicy? In order to be as clear and practical as possible, let us re-introduce an urgent and compelling case: Harold Kushner's son Aaron, who died of progeria at age fourteen. Kushner wants to know why Aaron had to suffer this dreadful disease, why Aaron had to be condemned to a life devoid of the blessings that other children received.[26] Kushner's own response is that God is loving and that God cares about Aaron and his parents, but that God did not have the power to prevent Aaron from suffering. God has power, but only the power to inspire people to be compassionate to fellow sufferers.

Is there a Christian response to theodicy that offers more comfort and wisdom than Kushner's own response? Yes, I am bold enough to believe there is. First of all, a Christian theodicy begins in the middle of things. Our light does not shine brightly enough to know where a terrible evil like progeria comes from. Its origins are shrouded in mystery. What we do know is that it does not come from God. God did not plant this weed; this devastation does not come from the hand of God. Aaron's disease was not only Aaron's enemy; it is God's enemy, too.

Second, we believe that when Kushner and his wife prayed for God to come into the midst of Aaron's suffering and to act, God answered their

---

26. Harold Kushner, *When Bad Things Happen to Good People* (New York: Avon, 1981), pp. 2-3.

prayer. God came as a warrior to do battle with the evil that had taken Aaron captive. But even though Kushner — and we — may have hoped that God would perform a miracle, would make war on the disease in conventional terms, swiftly wiping out every distorted strand of DNA, every vestige of the illness, God came instead to make war in God's own way. Kushner has decided that God came, but only in well-wishing impotence. But to the contrary, God came in tremendous power, but power consistent with the power of the God made known in Jesus Christ, power in the form of loving weakness. God's power was not a sword dividing good from evil; God's power was a mustard seed cast into a garden furrow, a small dash of yeast poured into an overwhelming volume of flour from the hand of an unnoticed woman. It is seemingly weak, insignificant, and hidden, and yet this power of love works inexorably to vanquish all evil. It is so unlike human exercises of power that we don't know how to see it, can hardly recognize it. God's power is so hidden, so disguised in weakness, that we despair that God is at work to combat evil at all. We lose faith in God because we have forgotten that "power is made perfect in weakness" (2 Cor. 12:9).

But Aaron Kushner suffered, and Aaron Kushner died. How can we say that God's power made perfect in weakness vanquished evil in Aaron's life? As we have said, it is cold comfort simply to say that Aaron is now in a better place, that Aaron now knows that evil has been defeated and that righteousness shines like the sun. What about those awful days of humiliation, fear, and suffering?

Here it is important to keep in view the image of God as a warrior — a warrior waging love, to be sure, but a warrior nonetheless. In Christ, the God of eternity, the God who transcends past, present, and future, enters all time and redeems it. Aaron suffered in his present, which has now, for him and for us, become the past. But the present and the past are not immune from the action of the eternal God. God invades the present and the past in love, and in God's own way destroys the work and power of evil. "The Greeks . . . thought that even the gods could not change the past," writes Frank Kermode, "but Christ did change it, rewrote it, and in a new way fulfilled it."[27]

---

27. Frank Kermode, *The Sense of an Ending: Studies in the Theory of Fiction with a New Epilogue* (New York: Oxford University Press, 2000), p. 47.

We cannot emphasize this claim enough. God in Christ does not say to Aaron and all other victims and human sufferers, "I know you had it hard in life, but now that you have experienced God's perfect and beatific reign, you can let bygones be bygones. Life in the kingdom makes all memory of suffering pale in comparison." No. The God revealed in Jesus Christ, in contrast, enters from eternity into time — from the future into the present and the past — and makes war on every seeming conquest of evil, even the conquest of our memories. Everything about evil — its vain and false claims of final victory, its pain caused in the present, its grip on our memory and our history — everything is thrown into the fire to be burned. Evil can claim no victories. It is unmasked as what it truly is . . . nothingness. The suffering Aaron experienced in his life — destroyed. The scars on his memory, and those borne by those who loved him — destroyed. The love of God does far more than place Aaron's suffering into proper context; it enters every chamber of Aaron's life — past, present, and future — and heals.

Much is known, of course, about the French war hero and head of state Charles de Gaulle. What is often not remembered about him was that he and his wife, Yvonne, were the parents of Anne, a child with Down syndrome. Every day, regardless of what was going on in the affairs of state, de Gaulle would come home and play tenderly with this child. Then he and Yvonne would put her to bed. Yvonne would often say, "Oh, Charles, why couldn't she have been like the others? I have prayed so often that she could have been like the others." Anne died before reaching full adulthood, and the family had a private graveside mass. When the mass was over, Yvonne was reluctant to leave the grave, reluctant to leave her beloved daughter. Charles rested his hand on Yvonne's arm and said to her, "Come, Yvonne. Now, she is like the others."

Coda: Pilgrim's Progress

The main purpose of this little book has been to think through what preachers can say, what teachers can teach, about the question of theodicy. Not everyone, of course, will agree with the positions I have taken, but in some ways that is beside the point. When we move beyond a "ministry of presence," when we dare to invite thoughtful Christians to engage intellectually with this urgent and complex theological issue, we convey our confidence that the Spirit will guide our minds into deeper communion with God.

But theodicy is more than a classroom matter. When we think clearly and well about what the God of Jesus Christ is doing in the world concerning evil and suffering, we are led to think also about how we, as people of faith, can join in with this divine work, even in a world of ambiguity and doubt. John L'Heureux has written an intriguing and troubling story titled "The Expert on God." The protagonist is a Jesuit priest who, from the age of ten, has been plagued by doubts — doubts about the Trinity, doubts about Christ's presence in the Eucharist, doubts about the virginity of Mary, doubts about the divinity of Christ, even doubts about the humanity of Christ. "At one time or another," the narrator tells us, "he doubted every article of belief, but only for a while, and only one at a time."[28]

Finally, however, he develops a doubt that will not pass: he begins to doubt the love of God. In the face of his doubt, he prays for faith, but none comes. So, he prays for hope, but when that is not given, either, he simply goes on with his duties — teaching, preaching, saying mass.

Then, one bright, clear day, after saying mass at Our Lady of Victories, he is driving home to the Jesuit house, marveling in his ironic and doubtful way over the absence of God in the world, when he comes across a terrible automobile accident. A young man lies dying, trapped in an overturned car. The priest is able to force open the crumpled car door and manages to cradle the man in his arms. Taking a vial of holy oil from his pocket, the priest anoints the dying man, pronouncing, "I ab-

---

28. John L'Heureux, "The Expert on God," in *Comedians* (New York: Penguin Books, 1990), p. 34.

solve you from all your sins. In the name of the Father and of the Son and of the Holy Ghost. Amen."

But, then, nothing happens. There is no shift in the world, no change in the dire situation, no word from heaven, not even any human rescuers. Only the silent world and the dying boy's "harsh, half-choked breathing." The priest begins to pray — recited prayers, rote prayers, prayers about Mary, prayers to the Father in heaven. He feels foolish, but what else can he do, what else can he say? Then come the final lines of the story, as the priest wonders what to do:

> What would God do at such a moment, if there were a God? "Well, do it," he said aloud, and heard the fury in his voice. "Say something." But there was silence from heaven.
>
> . . . What could anyone say to this crushed, dying thing, he wondered. What would God say if he cared as much as I? . . . The priest could see death beginning across the boy's face. And still he could say nothing.
>
> . . . The boy turned — some dying reflex — and his head tilted in the priest's arms, trusting, like a lover. And at once the priest, faithless, unrepentant, gave up his prayers and bent to him and whispered, fierce and burning, "I love you," and continued until there was no breath, "I love you, I love you, I love you."[29]

L'Heureux's character of the priest can be understood in two ways. Either he is finally the secular man who at last rids himself of the burden of his failed mythology and acts lovingly on his own, or — and this is my own wager — he is a converted man, a man who moves from a childish faith to a mature and hopeful one. In this latter view, the priest gives up his immature idea of a God who comes when we whistle to make everything all right in favor of a God who is at work in suffering as the hidden and loving warrior, summoning the faithful to join their actions with God's, calling them to be in the present world of pain what all humanity shall be in the end: those whose righteousness shines like the sun in the victorious love of God.

29. L'Heureux, "The Expert on God," p. 35.

Index

Index